Balls

Preface

Apparently, once the British had colonized India and established their businesses, they yearned for recreation and decided to build a golf course in Calcutta. Golf in Calcutta presented a unique obstacle. Monkeys would drop out of the trees, scurry across the course, and seize the balls. The monkeys would play with the balls, tossing them here and there, but rarely back on the fairways!

At first, the golfers tried to control the monkeys. Their first strategy was to build high fences around the fairways and greens. This approach, which seemed initially to hold much promise, was abandoned when the golfers discovered that a fence was no challenge to an ambitious monkey. Next the golfers tried luring the monkeys away from the course, but the monkeys found nothing as amusing as watching humans go wild whenever their little white balls were disturbed. In desperation, the British began trapping the monkeys. But for every monkey they carted off, another would appear. Finally, the golfers gave in to reality and developed a rather novel ground rule. <u>Play the ball where the monkey drops it.</u>

> …from a sermon by Rev. Dr. Gregory Knox Jones.

Our *balls* were dropped in the port town of Progreso on the Yucatan Peninsula – population, depending on which guidebook one reads, of twenty to forty thousand, *mas' o menos* the couple of hundred snowbirds who called it home each winter, flocking here to escape the harsh winters in Canada and the United States.

We were part of the Canadian flock. The larger of the two main migratory flocks, we outnumbered the gringo (American) flock by about two to one. On occasion, we spotted other species from as far away as Spain, Germany and New Zealand.

For every person whose *balls* are dropped here, there was a story. Let's face it. Most snowbirds migrated to Puerto Vallarta or Cancun, or, for the more conservative birds, Guadalajara and Lake Chapala, or San Miguel de Allende, north of Mexico City. There one could find whole flocks that speak English and never speak a word of Spanish all winter long. They ate American style food at American style restaurants, and watched American cable TV or read American newspapers and magazines.

The snowbirds here in Progreso were a very different breed, including us.

"How in the hell did two Canadian farm boys from Southern Ontario end up in the Yucatan Peninsula of México?" we were being asked for the umpteenth time. My initial response, as always, "Our balls were dropped here!"

Suffice to say that only made our questioner more curious. What invariably followed was the *Reader's Digest* version of our lives up to this point –

1. Indeed we were two farm boys from Ontario.
2. We were both previously teachers.
3. Both of us had been married, John for 32 years and myself for 38 years.
4. Each of us had two grown children, John with two boys and me with two girls. I had five grandchildren and one great granddaughter; John had one grandson.
5. Towards the end of our respective marriages we both had begun to explore Internet chat sites, eventually gay chat lines.
6. We came to realize that we were indeed gay!
7. In 2004, we left Ontario, Canada and travelled over 3000 kilometers to Progreso, a place we would eventually come to call home.

And now, as the late *Paul Harvey* would say, "Here is the rest of the story."

***

I guess you might say that our *balls* were first dropped in our respective mothers' wombs – sixty some years ago. We would like to say that we were both much younger than sixty - *mas joven* as they say in Spanish, but the truth is that we were actually only eighteen months apart. John was a pre-boomer (1944) and I was a boomer (1945).

There were lots of things we had in common aside from being gay. John was adopted shortly after he was born. I liked to tease my mother that I too must have been adopted since I thought I was unlike either of my parents. So I thought in my younger years. As time went by, the resemblance in the mirror was stronger...

I had an older sister by four years. John was an only child to his adoptive parents. In some ways that probably accounted for him loving to be the centre of attention in social gatherings...one place we were very different. I had always been shy and self-conscious, until I got to know people better.

We were raised on farms, albeit hundreds of miles apart in Ontario, Canada. Whereas John's adoptive father was a more conservative farmer who used traditional equipment, my father was always up-to-date, using the most recent technologies and machinery. He was also more prosperous, or so it seemed.

John's father had various livestock – chickens, pigs, cattle; our farm had primarily Holstein cattle, although I do remember some chickens when I was very young. Embedded in my mind was the image of someone putting a chicken's head between two nails on a tree stump and then chopping its head off, after which its bloodied carcass flopped around in a circle until it finally succumbed to its fate. Amazingly, I still eat chicken!

(John had similar experiences with chickens on his farm. This training, at his father's side, would later be used to secure a fine Christmas duck in for our first Christmas together outside of Canada.)

For the better part of John's father's life he farmed. My father had other interests at various times. He drove the big yellow school bus which took my sister and me to the consolidated rural school every day. In the summer, he played on a traveling baseball team (mostly Sundays when farm work was put on hold). Once a month, on Saturday nights he would play the drums in a small trio at the community hall at the end of our rural road. In addition, he was a volunteer fireman, and for a period of time, a township councillor. Looking back, it was hard to remember when he ever spent much time at home, except to eat and sleep.

Towards the end of my parents' sixteen year marriage, my father had an affair with our nineteen year old babysitter. Conveniently, she lived on the farm behind ours on the next concession. It started to take him longer to take her home after she sat us. My mother eventually confronted him. Being young at the time, I never thought about sex, let alone my father having a sexual relationship with our sitter. Actually, until this moment I cannot say I ever pictured him doing that with her or my mother. I got yelled at once for opening the bathroom door when he was getting out of the tub... *was that the moment when my desire to see naked men began?* Some would argue that one becomes gay – environmental factors are at play...distant or absent father, prudishness, etc. *I do not subscribe to that theory.* I believe being gay is a genetic disposition, and yet I know of no other gays or lesbians hanging from our family tree. My mother was an only child and my father had ten brothers and sisters, all seemingly straight, as are all of my cousins to my knowledge.

When my parents separated and subsequently divorced, I rarely saw my father. He moved 125 miles away to stay with his younger brother. Once he was settled, and my sixteen year old sister went to live with him, his visits to the farm (which he had secretly sold to his younger brother) were very infrequent.

Our mothers were typical farm wives from all accounts – cooking, baking, cleaning, washing, etc. Each belonged to the Women's Institute – an organization of like-minded Canadian farm wives. My mother liked to play euchre with the neighbouring women once a week. John's parents neither played cards nor drank alcoholic beverages. He grew up in a God-fearing home! His mother belonged to the Temperance Union and the Women's Missionary Society.

At an early age we both took piano lessons (likely not our fathers' first choice for their son). My interest waned quickly. John went on to win many awards for his capabilities right on up into university. I switched to vocal music and won many awards at the annual music festival. We were choir boys in the United Church (known as

Methodist in the United States). Neither of us was athletic in our youth, but I did try Little League one summer to appease my father. OUCH! That *ball* was hard...so un-Canadian, eh? I never played hockey either, although I did own a pair of secondhand ice skates. Does it count that I collected hockey trading cards of the NHL, back when there were only six teams – Montreal, Toronto, Boston, Detroit, New York and Chicago?

John grew up next door to his future wife; I met mine when I attended high school in the nearby town. Both of us would marry our best friend – the first real girlfriends that either of us had.

For me, and to some extent John, marriage was an expectation for young men in the sixties. In adolescence, John had a few heterosexual experiences, but absolutely NO same sex experiences. While I had a girlfriend, I continued for a short period during my high school years to have ONLY same sex experiences (mainly with a slightly older cousin), although increasingly infrequent. Sex with my girlfriend (future wife) only occurred after marriage.

Eventually, my mother and I moved one hundred miles away from the farm. She had been transferred by her work for a national grocery chain. By this time, my parents had finally divorced and she had taken work as a cashier. With my cousin one hundred miles away, same sex activity ceased, but not the desires.

My girlfriend and I broke up that year. When my mother was transferred back to my hometown, my girlfriend and I reconnected in college. That summer, after my first year in college, my father died unexpectedly. Since I had not seen him for a few years, the real impact of his death was not felt until many years later. I completed college and started to work. We got engaged at Christmas and were married the following summer. Societal expectations never entered my mind. I truly did want to spend the rest of my life with her.

John and his girlfriend had a slightly longer courtship and were married two years later. They had both gone to university. Ironically, we had both chosen the same careers – teaching. John's wife became a nurse.

John came out of the closet seven or eight years before me. His circle of friends was led to believe that he and his wife had become incompatible – a story with which his wife felt comfortable. No woman wants to admit that she has been cast aside for a man. It would have been unheard of at that time.

To a great degree, the Internet played a large part in both acceptance of being gay. We had both discovered gay chat rooms. In the beginning we had each chatted with other men online – many of them married like us. Building up our courage we both advanced to actually meeting the men with whom we chatted. John's first encounter was with a real estate agent in a secluded wood near his home. Mine was with a real estate agent in my own home while my wife was at work. He was much older than I expected (aren't they all?) and walked in with his briefcase just in case anyone saw him. He wasted no time with pleasantries, quickly undressing and letting his intentions be known. It was not a satisfying experience. I almost laughed out loud at the red bikini underwear he was wearing.

John and I both experimented with men at various times. He would eventually settle with one man after he left his wife. Coincidentally, this man – Jack, had recently been divorced as well. While they were together, I suspected that John also saw other men while Jack was at work. At least one of them was not committed...

Early on, I had begun to chat with a twenty-two year old guy from a mid-western state – Chris. This eventually led to nightly conversations on the chat line, while my wife was asleep upstairs. There were occasional telephone calls from public telephones. Neither of us had web cams. I became very emotionally attached to him. I gave serious thought to leaving my wife and going to see him at one point.

Ultimately, he told me that he had been diagnosed with stomach cancer. I was devastated. Not long after, I received an email from his friend informing me that Chris had been admitted to hospital. I went into denial. All would be well. I would eventually be able to meet him face to face. I remained positive about the outcome...

While my wife was working, I spent hours in the gay chat rooms. One afternoon I met a man who convinced me to meet him at the city's only gay bath house – an experience I will never forget.

After that seamy experience, I had second thoughts about being gay. I was ashamed, but more so afraid of what I had done. What disease might I have picked up? I lived in fear for several days…and then went online once again – more men, more secluded meetings. After that, I found a small motel (no questions asked) where I conducted my frequent rendezvous. I also learned to meet the guys first in public coffee shops. No more blind dates! Canadian cities are notorious for coffee shops on every corner.

In the course of eight weeks my world had been turned inside out. I was living secretly for my next sexual encounter with a stranger. I actually lost track of how many men I was with in those first two months. Almost all were brief encounters and one night stands.

I became desperate – I was spiraling downward. In my desperation, I confided in my family doctor. I held back on the sexual details, letting on that I was severely depressed and potentially suicidal. He sent me directly to the Crisis Center at the local hospital (Catholic). I was interviewed by a psychiatrist immediately. Holding back nothing, I needed to unburden myself at last; my wife was called. I was admitted immediately to the psychiatric ward. I was locked in a private room for seventy-two hours – no clothes, no toiletries, no books to read, no music. Occasional visits from a doctor or nurse and lots of medications and blood tests. I was shocked when a doctor suggested an HIV test. Had I gone this far down the proverbial rabbit hole?

My wife and family were led to believe that my depression was rooted in my father's absence from my childhood home, subsequent divorce and untimely death at age forty-two. Only my nurses and doctors in the hospital knew the whole truth. I knew that they were sworn to respect my privacy.

One nurse in particular really 'abused' me emotionally. How could I subject my wife to the potential of a sexually transmitted disease? Eventually I was moved into a step-down unit where I had contact with other patients. They were all ages, male and female. One guy had overdosed during an orgy with women while using poppers. Another was raising four young children whose mother had burned to death in a house fire five months before. He and his wife had been married only a little over a year. The extra responsibility had sent him there, as they were totally unprepared for it, emotionally as well as financially. The younger patients included a nymphomaniac and numerous drug abusers. One of the older women had driven her car into a tree in her own driveway attempting to kill herself. She totally destroyed the car, but wasn't successful with her suicide. Now she was fighting daily on the telephone with her insurance company to get her car repaired! Talk about balls?

We were all heavily sedated and had daily routines to follow. After one week I was allowed to wear my own clothes and shave with a razor. I was allowed visitors off the floor, so I was finally able to see my grandchildren. When the HIV test results came back negative I was finally released – thirteen days in all.

As soon as I was released from the hospital I was back in the chat room. I had no contact with Chris, but did send him an email describing what I had been through since last we were able to chat. There was no reply.

Nothing changed until that fateful day when my wife came home from work unexpectedly and found me in bed with another man. My secret was out. I felt liberated, but understood fully that my marriage was now doomed – divorce was inevitable. How? When? I packed my clothes and went by taxi to a nearby motel. At the motel I called another friend who came over. He advised me to go home and work it out. I called my wife so that she would know I was safe. She asked if she could come over and talk. I agreed. I admitted all that had transpired over the last month, including the details about Chris and why I had been in the hospital. Now she knew the whole truth!

Eventually, my wife and I agreed on the terms of an open relationship. I would continue to see men OUTSIDE our home if that is what I wanted, but not on weekends. That was family time. (By this time both of my daughters were married and had children of their own). I would always play safe. I told her about my HIV results. I would tell her who I was going out with in case I got into trouble (first names only), of course. What I was doing involved great risks – physically. I never considered how great a toll the emotional roller coaster would have. Our grown daughters would not be told anything until such time as we could work this through.

In early November I received another email from Chris' friend informing me that Chris had gone into a coma following surgery and died!!!! I was shattered. I had lost what I had thought was my best friend ever! Who could I turn to who would understand what I was going through?

Just before Christmas I met Jack in the chat room – *the* Jack, John's partner.

By now the two of them were separated. John had gone off to Mexico after retiring, leaving Jack behind in Canada. Jack was still working and not retired. John was in Progreso teaching English as a Second Language. Jack and I met at a local coffee shop one day, before returning to his apartment, the one he had shared with John. There, in *their* bed, we involved ourselves in the usual man to man activities which I had come to enjoy with other men.

When I first met Jack I was not attracted to him. For a couple of weeks, I ignored his invitations, choosing to spend my leisure time with other guys. I was always attracted to men in their thirties…Jack was almost the same age as I was. His was NOT the body of a thirty year old, but then neither was mine as a matter of fact!

By this time I had found a counselor, an ex-priest who had come out of the closet a few years earlier. We talked at length about my childhood, my career, my family and my father, as well as the men I had seen or was seeing, and, of course,

Chris. Once a week there was group therapy with two other guys – one was out and the other was closeted to his family – European background. I wrestled with being gay after all those years. The counselor listened without judgment. Had it not been for his compassion and understanding I might have ended up back in the psychiatric ward or worse.

Christmas came and went and I continued to see Jack and to discuss my dilemma. He had been married and could appreciate where I was at in my process of coming out. We would see each other once more before my wife and I left for our annual six week stay in the Florida Panhandle, south of Alabama, in late January 2004 (just three months after my hospitalization).

In a sense it was to be a retreat – time to work out our future, together or apart. Realistically, the chances of maintaining a marriage under these circumstances were less than ten percent. I had done some reading. My wife and I had both read several books offered by my counselor. Without Jack to chat with I felt so alone. I had begun a journal at the suggestion of my counselor. I made the decision to share it with my wife as a starting point in our discussions. Details were there – grounds for divorce. The unspeakable acts of the previous six months were now fully out in the open. No more lies. She finally knew the truth of what I had been doing before she found me in bed that fateful afternoon. She knew about Jack, but was never to meet him.

No doubt shattered by the unvarnished truth, she agreed that I should call him, one afternoon from

Florida. What had begun as a sexual liaison had by now evolved into a patient-counselor relationship. I needed to talk with someone. Jack had made a decision to become a minister with his church. Our relationship had to change. Still, he continued to be my confidant – my big brother (even though he was younger). We had no secrets. He knew about Chris and his untimely death. Together we held a memorial "balloon ceremony" one evening in a nearby park where I finally decided that I had to let Chris go.

Six weeks after arriving back in Canada I was off to Toronto for a weekend of discovery. I had wanted Jack to go with me, but he declined. There were limited opportunities to meet gay men publicly in our small blue-collar city. My wife had encouraged me to go, much to my surprise. Traveling by train, I arrived in Toronto and found a hotel room not far from the gay village on Church Street. I proceeded to explore the various clubs and bars. My heart raced each time I entered a new one, but in the end, they were all the same – meat markets. What did I expect? I did not see me in the faces of any of the men there. They were all in their early twenties or thirties. Where were the men my age? Were they all dead or dying from AIDS? Early on, my counselor had said that had I come out earlier, I might well have died from AIDS by now.

Was I destined to spend the rest of my life in seedy dance clubs and bars, paying for 'adventures' with younger men?

Returning home on the train the next morning I reflected on my experiences...maybe I was truly bisexual. I couldn't see myself living the rest of my life like this. I did love my wife. Perhaps I truly was having a mid-life crisis?

I continued to meet with Jack – *sans* sex, just long discussions about where I was headed. To make up for the lack of physical intimacy, I turned to the chat room and met Craig, a man in his mid to late twenties who lived about twenty minutes away. I always visited him after dark, covertly going to his door – his parents lived right next door and shared a driveway! Our times together were great. I made the mistake of getting too attached...too soon. My age wasn't a factor for him. He felt safe. We were very discreet, never seeing each other in public. We had no contact outside his house. I seriously considered that we might become a couple. I wanted him to go away with me, if only for weekends. He wasn't prepared for that at this stage of his life. I understood. He was still very closeted, even with his own family.

At the end of June, while I was seeing Craig, I was still talking with Jack. His partner John was returning from Mexico. There was to be a party to which we were all invited. Aside from Craig, I was still seeing other guys occasionally. On the day of the party I finally met John for the first time. There was something about him which intrigued me. He had an air of confidence about him. I was a little uneasy that night. What did he really know about Jack and me? A few nights later, I met he and Jack at another event. At one point in the evening I felt his hand on my knee. I wondered what that was all about.

The seating arrangement at the restaurant for dinner was pretty funny, like a scene from a Woody Allen movie. There was myself, then John, then Jack and then another friend, Ralph. Jack purposefully sat John between us because Ralph had a previous short-lived affair with John. Talk about your triangles…we were a quadrilateral! Jack didn't want them sitting together. Little did he realize at the time that he set in motion John and my eventual coming together two weeks later.

One week after I met John, he and Jack headed west to get Jack set up in his new apartment at the college where he was to be studying for the ministry. I was distraught when I didn't hear from Jack for over a week. And then…I received an IM from John! He was heading back to Canada. Could we meet for dinner and get better acquainted? According to Jack's plan, John was to take over his role as mentor and friend. I wasn't sure he ever could be at that time.

When John arrived home he called. How about dinner at the apartment? Actually it was Jack's apartment. He had agreed to let John stay on until he left again for Mexico at the end of September. It seemed the friendly thing to do. I said that I would bring the wine. We agreed on Greek takeout from a restaurant beside the building. It was the same place and same food that Jack and I used to have – gyros, Greek salad and wine.

Sitting on the balcony we talked and ate and drank red wine…very sociable. I really had no male friends, just co-workers. I was open to a friendship. I didn't expect what followed...

As the sun set and the temperatures dropped, we moved inside to a warmer place. I sat on Jack's couch and was surprised when John sat right beside me. Without hesitation he reached over and put his hand on my knee for the second time. Remember the dinner? He proceeded to kiss me. I made no attempt to stop him and before long we were in the bed which he and Jack had shared before he had moved to Mexico. It was the same bed that Jack and I shared in the beginning of our relationship. This was totally unexpected, although I did learn later that John had more or less planned it all! This wasn't supposed to happen! I still wanted a relationship with Craig!

A few weeks later, when my counselor and I talked about it, I finally came to realize the irrationality of continuing with Craig. I needed to end it. He wasn't about to commit to someone twice his age...okay two and one-half times his age. I tried to call him, but he didn't answer. I wrote him a long email explaining my decision – it was over. I hoped that we could remain friends after all this. There would be no more sexual trysts late at night. He sent back a short reply abiding by my decision, leaving the doors open to future adventures should they occur.

In mid-March, with my wife seated beside me in our family room, I told my two daughters and their husbands that I was gay. They were shocked, but over the course of the next few days, they came to accept the inevitable.

What I thought might be an occasional diversion with John proceeded with regularity. After dinner with my wife, I would head over to John's apartment to play and chat, usually returning before my wife went to bed. We were still sleeping in the same bed. John and my sexual experimentation advanced quickly. He was more experienced than I having been out for seven years. I introduced John to my wife three weeks later! I felt that she needed to know whom I was seeing, hoping she would be reassured that he wasn't some sex-crazed twenty something after my money. What money? I also wanted her to know that I wasn't being promiscuous any more. For all appearances John was a 'normal' guy. Over breakfast at a local restaurant, John and I sat across from her and had a civilized conversation – no animosity, no tears, and no harsh words. It went surprisingly well. I think he and I were both shocked, especially when she gave him a big hug on leaving the restaurant. That would set the tone for our remaining weeks together as a married couple. Civility. There were never any angry shouting matches...

John and I continued to meet regularly, almost daily depending on my work schedule. We went for bike rides in the country and shared picnic lunches by the lake. I felt very special when he would bring me lunch at work sometimes when he wasn't busy. I often worried that he might be playing with some other guy while I was working. I had no way of knowing for sure without asking. I didn't. From time to time we had a threesome at the apartment. John had seen two other guys before we met. He thought it might be fun to get together with one in particular – a married guy, not out, but aggressive in bed. We invited him over a few times and we all enjoyed ourselves. One time we invited a younger guy over. We had an agreement about how far we would go beforehand.

Sometimes when we were together at the apartment, Jack would call. That was strange. John never let on that he was seeing me. I usually went out onto the balcony to give them privacy.

On occasion when I was there, John would chat online with his friend, Arturo, in Mexico. They had a relationship before John returned to Canada. John was hoping to get Arturo to Canada during his stay. In the beginning, that didn't bother me. John and I were not partners. If he wanted Arturo in Canada, that was his choice. Eventually, Arturo stopped chatting with John. I can only surmise that he understood well what was going on between John and me.

One night after I had gone home, John invited a guy whom I knew and had been with a few times, to come over. When he told me about it I was furious. In retaliation, I went out and did the same thing with another guy. After that we agreed not to play one on one with anyone else unless we were together! For me, that was a real challenge!

Eventually I told my wife that I wanted to spend the night with John. It wasn't just the sex. I wanted to know male love in all its' permutations. Was this what I wanted for the rest of my life? She agreed, although I couldn't imagine what went through her mind that night as she lay awake, alone, in our bed, knowing that her husband of thirty-eight years was likely having some type of sex at that very moment with another man. What would she visualize us doing together?

What occurred between John and me that first night was more than enough to convince me that he was the one with whom I wanted to spend the rest of my life. I actually fell asleep in his arms – something I had never done with my wife! I awoke in a dream world – for the first time in my life, there was a man lying next to me when I opened my eyes to the morning light. Within three weeks my wife and I separated and I moved in with John. Jack was still in the dark about us. My decision was irrevocable. We told my daughters. I packed my clothes and told our closest friends and neighbors what was transpiring. I admitted being gay. I wanted no lies. Obviously they were saddened as well as shocked. We had seemed to have the perfect suburban marriage.

From the start, John and I promised to communicate openly and fully. It was a new experience for me. He told me all about his past – his wife, his two boys, his various affairs, including the recent one in Mexico with Arturo, the thirty-something Mexican architect. We adjusted to our new life together, sharing closets (clothes, that is) and household duties. We took a one week vacation and went camping in a national park in northern Ontario. It was a new experience for me. Camping, hiking and canoeing occupied our days. We canoed and skinny dipped in the cold, Northern waters. It felt like a honeymoon…When we returned we announced to my wife and daughters that he and I were heading south to Mexico for a month. I promised John that I would try living there until just before Christmas and then decide whether or not to return with him after Christmas. I looked upon it as a trial, a new start for him and me…together.

I continued to think about Chris and spent many hours with my counselor working through the other problems before we headed to Mexico.

One day, while surfing the net, I 'Googled' Chris' name. Imagine my surprise when I found a recent mention! He was alive, or so it appeared…

I sent an email to Chris' friend who explained that Chris was alive but paralyzed from the surgery to control the cancer. It had been Chris' idea to tell me that he had died to break off the relationship! More shattering news…

I emailed Chris and finally got a response. He still remembered me, of course. He had forgotten some of the details of our relationship as a result of the coma. I was thankful that he was alive! I knew that the relationship could not be rebuilt, no matter how much I wanted it to be like old times. I spoke by telephone with him one last time when I went on a retreat to the Midwest. He was moving to Montana with his friend to start over. He was slowly learning to walk again…was this more fiction? I would never know. Looking back after several years, I sometimes wonder if there ever really was a Chris or was it my Spirit communicating with me to assist me in my coming out process? Had he sent me a guide?

I had gone west to take some spiritual enlightenment courses, leaving John to pack our belongings. When I returned to Canada, John drove west to take the course too. At the end of his courses, I took a train from Detroit to meet him prior to the drive south to Mexico. As the train passed across the Midwest, I was inspired to write my first ever poem, which expressed what I was feeling at that moment in my life –

JOY

In the darkness of my life
Uncertainty held firmly onto my heart
And mind.
There was no light, no beacon
My soul perceived the sunset
Alone.

Unexpectedly
The sunset became dawn
And in the mist of morning
You appeared.
First a glimmer
And then a touch.
My body, my mind, my heart
Strained to understand.

Some would have me believe
Too soon…not right…wrong person
For me.

I reached for your hand

You took hold of my heart.
We tasted and tested love
Not for the first time...
We both carried
The baggage of our past
Divine guidance?
Sinful love?

Naked
We looked into each other's souls
And reached out our hands, our minds,
Our hearts...and looked into the mirrors of our
eyes
To accept God's love
And I found the elusive
Joy.

Eight hours later, I got off the train and walked into John's arms. In the seclusion of the parking lot he embraced me and we shared a long kiss. This was no longer a dream!

By the time we got to the Mexican border we knew this was right for both of us. We still had to deal with Jack's feelings of betrayal on both our parts. I told John that I would give him one gift before we left Canada for Mexico – the gift of *time* – time to work out a new relationship with Jack on a different level. We would also need time to adjust to being together 24/7 since I would not be working. We would be living in a foreign country where neither of us spoke the language at the time. There would be major adjustments.

Seven days after leaving Canada, we arrived in Progreso. Our *balls* had been dropped. This was where we would start our new life together.

Over the years others would drop their balls in our area of Mexico. The following are *their* stories...

***

George and Alyce had purchased their hotel just prior to the onslaught of Hurricane Isidora in 2002. Alyce had been a psychologist in Canada – three times married. George was originally, according to his official biography – an economist turned entrepreneur. A man in his early sixties, owning a hotel/bar was no doubt the reason he looked older. Alcohol has a way of aging one's face and body! They had two teenaged children.

They were a key factor in John's being in Progreso in the first place. Besides the hotel, they operated an English as a Foreign Language school for Mexicans, including the towns police department. Progreso had long been a mecca for Canadian and American snowbirds. Several cruise ships called weekly, bringing thousands more tourists to the town. For the most part they left for the Maya ruins of nearby Chichen Itza or Uxmal. Those who stayed and played on the beach were the responsibility of the tourist police. It was for this reason that the tourist police studied English. The TP were responsible for patrolling the waterfront – miles of public beach, known as the *malecon.*

In 2003, while still in Canada and in the process of ending his six year relationship with Jack, John had taken a TESOL course in Canada. George and Alyce offered to people who had taken the course, an opportunity to practice what they had learned. Seeing an opportunity to visit Mexico for the first time, John accepted their offer. He would teach English to a small group of Mexican students in return for an honorarium of four hundred pesos per week, lodging and meals. He already was collecting a pension from his earlier teaching job; this was a chance to see Mexico – the real Mexico. Eventually he hoped to go to Japan or Korea or maybe China...without Jack.

He arrived in September for his three week stint, and was assigned his first classes. He shared a small *casita* (house) not far from the hotel with four other 'teachers' one Mexican male, one French-Canadian male and two Canadian females. In the small casita behind their casa lived the Mexican, who was more or less in charge of the other teachers, even though he was much younger. On occasion he would have male guests who stayed overnight. Yes, he was gay. In the beginning, John never offered that he was also gay, but little by little those details emerged.

For John it was a wonderful experience in the beginning. He fell in love with Progreso and Mexico. His 'kids' the other teachers and honorary teachers, though much younger, accepted him as a peer, and maybe a substitute father in some ways.

During those first weeks in Progreso he quietly pursued his interests in men using local Internet chat rooms. He never actually divulged being gay to his employers, George and Alyce. After all, he was working predominately with adolescent males and females. He was their teacher! Any socializing he did was away from the school in the city nearby, far from prying eyes.

It was made very clear from the outset that the teachers' conduct outside the school had to be above reproach, both male and female. Alyce had eyes and ears all around the town. Ok, they were her spies. One evening, the young, male Mexican teacher invited another Mexican guy to stay the night. He was introduced to John. Subsequently, the two Mexicans went back to the casita. The lights were dimmed and the curtains drawn. From his room, John could hear their voices. It was very clear that they were not watching TV. John fully recognized the sounds coming from the casita! Then there was silence. After that incident, no visitors were allowed in the casita overnight. Somehow Alyce had found out! Those spies were well paid...

John returned home after those first six weeks but agreed to return in January as a full-time teacher. The circumstances at the school had changed. Other Canadians arrived for the three week practicum. Eventually, the Mexicans became unhappy that they hadn't received their expected Christmas bonuses. The utilities commission had shut down the first school when it was discovered that George and Alyce had someone 'rig' the electric meters so they were receiving free electricity to run the air conditioners. They were fined 90,000 pesos, about eight thousand US dollars in 2005. After the school was shut down, classes were conducted in the upper rooms of the hotel, near the beach. Meanwhile, George and Alyce continued to advertise the program and the hotel on their Internet website.

John had enough of their childish rules and found his own place in town – the place where we were now living. He still taught at the school and took his meals, but living alone, he was free to socialize with whomever he pleased. His most frequent visitor was the young architect, Arturo. If he chose to spend the night, John didn't need to worry about Alyce and George or the school's reputation. In fact, Arturo had been at the casa on several occasions. Sometimes he would spend the night with John. John was a grown man who didn't take to being treated like one of George and Alyce's teenage children. At the end of the school year John returned to Canada vowing not to work for George and Alyce ever again. He was keen to return to Progreso as he had made many good friends, both Mexican and foreigners.

On his first day home in Canada, we met at Jack's going away party. The fallout from that meeting resulted in our respective *balls* dropping in Progreso four months later.

We arrived in Progreso late in the evening after a fourteen hour ride from near Cordoba. The landlord was not at the casa. John did not yet have the keys to get in. Hungry and tired, we went to the nearby hotel (George & Alyce's) for something to eat. John had left on good terms in

June. Since it was not far from our new place, we could call the landlord for the keys and get something to eat quickly and call it a night. Of course, I was introduced to George and Alyce. We exchanged pleasantries and ate our meal – *sopa de lima* – Mexican soup. I had no first impressions of them. They seemed nice enough – at least they spoke English. I had real concerns about being able to communicate here in Spanish – I knew absolutely no Spanish except what I picked up at Taco Bell!

We finally reached the landlord on his cell phone and got the keys. Our *casa* was about eight blocks from the hotel. One block from the beach, it was on a quiet sandy street and was surrounded by tropical trees – crotons, almendres and bougainvillea. Of course, I did not see those until the morning. It was dark outside. We unpacked sheets and pillows and went straight to sleep AFTER killing two cockroaches we found in the kitchen and bathroom! Unpacking all of our worldly possessions would wait. They were securely locked in John's Toyota 4RnR. On the drive down from the US, there had been barely room for me to sit in the front seat amid all of the various boxes and clothes and small appliances – almost all of our worldly possessions, except the winter clothing that we had left behind in a friend's attic in Canada.

***

We flew back to Canada mid-December and were met at the airport by my wife and two grand daughters. It was strange...I got to drive my own car again...with my wife beside me in the passenger seat and John in the back seat with my grandkids.

John and I had previously agreed that we would be apart that Christmas. Jack's family was expecting them as they were not aware of the break up of the relationship yet. Likewise Jack's grown children in Canada did not yet know. He and John were traveling north to stay with Jack's brother and to have their usual family Christmas one last time. This was the norm all the years that they were together. Jack's elderly mother would be there as would several nieces and nephews.

I had made plans to stay at my oldest daughter's home for a few days and was then going to spend a week at my friend Geoff's condo overlooking the river. For part of the time, I would be alone while Geoff went out of town to visit his mother. I was the official house sitter.

For a few days, John and I did spend time together finishing our Christmas shopping. The first Saturday night, my daughter was hosting an open house for friends, business associates and family. Since my wife was to be there, John was NOT invited! When my wife found out she immediately called my daughter and let her know that she had no problems with John and I both attending. It was hard to believe that this was less than three months since I had left the marital house?

We arrived at the party before my wife did and were cordially greeted by my son-in-law's family who were already there – his parents, his brothers and his grandmother. I introduced John to each of them. Other friends greeted us as well. My wife arrived about an hour later. When she walked in she greeted everyone and then came over and hugged both John and I. Talk about *balls*? My daughter's mother-in-law's mouth dropped open in shock! She no doubt thought my wife must be crazy. The evening ended with John driving back to stay at another friend's house - a woman from our church – Louise. While I was at my daughter's, he was staying there. We had thought it too soon to be sleeping together at our friend's place. She was also a good friend of Jack's.

Before I fell asleep I called John's cell phone. He had spoken to Louise. She had no problem with us sleeping at her house. Would I come over to spend the night with him? Dumb question. Off I went.

Winters in Canada can be cold in an old house near the river. There was some snow on the ground. It was quite cold – all the more reason to snuggle under the blankets. We hadn't done that for a while in the heat of Mexico...finally we both fell asleep in each others' arms.

Two days before Christmas John headed north in a rental car. Jack was driving his own and had gone ahead. I was relieved. Once they got to their destination I would start to worry again. My sense of insecurity always managed to rear its' ugly head.

I moved over to Geoff's condo with him the day that John left. I had known Geoff for about six months before John and I left for Mexico. He was in his late thirties, single and, yes, gay. We had never really had a sexual relationship, choosing instead to spend time talking over coffee or going out for lunch or drinks. I wasn't his type! He was definitely not mine, even though he was the right age according to my criteria. He was like a skateboarder who had never grown up. He preferred 'twinks' – teenage boys.

One often has friends different from themselves. He was a good friend and a good listener. I had only been to his condo once before for a birthday party with a few other gay guys of various ages. I was comfortable with the plans we had made. While I was there we would share his king size bed – no sex! I cooked the meals and generally kept the condo clean, doing some laundry for the two of us while he was at work in one of the cities' many automotive plants.

Geoff left on Christmas Eve morning. That evening I went to my wife's house for our traditional get together with my daughters' children and spouses. It was strange driving back to Geoff's place afterwards. My wife let me use 'our' van.

When I awoke it was Christmas Day. A blanket of snow had fallen as I looked out across the river. It was beautiful! A White Christmas! I was alone on Christmas morning for the first time in my whole life! Of course I was emotional. I needed John. He was five hours away with his ex-partner. We had agreed not to telephone each other. Jack's brother would wonder what was going on.

After getting dressed, I went to pick up my elderly mother. Her apartment was actually two blocks from Geoff's condo. We drove to my wife's again for Christmas dinner with the family. After dinner I drove my elderly mother home and went back to the condo.

John and Jack returned in their respective cars on Boxing Day. John called me when he reached the outskirts of the city. He and Jack were stopping for coffee first. My mind wandered as always. Was it just coffee? There was a small 'no questions' motel near the coffee shop. *I outta know.*

That night we made up for lost time as they say, watching videos, using Geoff's Jacuzzi, again surrounded by candles. This time we drank red wine as we listened to soft music. Then, for the first time in several days, we went to bed together – our Christmas. We vowed that New Year's Eve would be our time.

Two days later Jack returned to his school, but not before the three of us sat down for a long awaited discussion of our respective futures. John and I both wanted to remain Jack's friend if he could come to terms with us. He was still bitter and hurt, but we all tried to remain calm and not raise our voices. Jack decided that what was best for him was to break off all communications with us for six months. He needed time. We concurred. Secretly, I knew he could not help but communicate with John for six days let alone six months. They had almost seven years together. That doesn't dissolve overnight. John wasn't ready to let go totally either. I tried to be pragmatic about the whole situation.

New Year's Eve arrived. Our friends had invited us to spend the evening at one's house. It wasn't what we wanted, but we agreed and ushered in 2005 with all of the people in New York City's Times Square via television as well as Ralph, Jeff and Louise – our closest friends.

Two weeks later, my oldest daughter drove us back to the airport for our flight back to Mexico. Hopefully the next Christmas would be different – less painful for all of us. When we arrived back in Mexico later that night we took a cab to Tom and Frank's place in the city. We were too exhausted to head back to Progreso.

***

John had met Tom online while we were still in Canada. Tom had told him to keep in touch when we got to Progreso. Shortly after arriving we accepted their invitation to dinner with some other gay friends and Tom's partner, also an American, although slightly older than us.

Tom and Frank, his partner of eighteen years had originally come down on vacation. Like many others, they fell in love with the place, coming back six months later with Frank's aging mother, to purchase an old casa which they had now remodeled. Originally from New Orleans, their *balls* too had been dropped in Mexico. Both had been married – Tom with one son and Frank with two children – a boy and a girl. In spite of their divorces, they were both better off financially than John and I. It was obvious. And yet, they were very down to earth guys. Frank spoke fluent Spanish, as his mother had been born in South America. In New Orleans, Tom was into marketing, while Frank was in communications. They invited us to stay over that first night. John and I agreed that Tom and Frank would only ever be friends, even though I harbored beliefs that John was attracted to Tom for some unknown reason. I wasn't privy to their prior conversations.

Funny, as a couple, they were very much like John and I. I am sure people thought it strange that John and I were partners. John was almost six feet tall and slender, except for his muscular chest. I was five foot six and a little chubby – middle age spread had taken its toll. We considered ourselves 'complementary', both in our daily lives and in bed. Tom and Frank appeared very similar to us in that regard. In any gay relationship, one partner always seems to have more feminine characteristics than another. Somebody has to cook…

So here we were, two months after meeting them again, staying overnight again. In the morning we returned by taxi, to Progreso, heading to our usual hotel for breakfast. It was good to be back 'home', for we had decided that this was HOME. From now on we would vacation in Canada, but live in Mexico, as long as we possibly could.

***

It was almost time for John's sixty-first birthday. We had decided to purchase commitment rings by then. Traveling into the city we ordered handmade matching gold and silver bands. While we were walking around we decided on getting tattoos. We had been discussing it for some time. As a father I hated the fact that my youngest daughter had several – some visible. John had three already – interwoven bands on each of his biceps and a circle of fishes around his ankle. I should also mention that his left nipple was also pierced!

What the hell! I would do it. I selected a smallish figure –*Kokopelli* – a Hopi Indian symbol of fertility and joy. One hour later, I left with my first tattoo on my right calf. John had a similar, but larger Kokopelli tattooed on his left calf.

The year before, John had celebrated his sixtieth birthday with the other young teachers from the school when he was first in Progreso. I wanted to have the other teachers over for drinks and appetizers that year. One thing led to another and the next thing I knew we had thirty-five people – straight and gay, young and old, Mexicans, Americans and Canadians for a Texas style BBQ around the corner at the hotel. The owner agreed to do the barbecuing – Texas brisket and ribs smoked over a slow fire. Of course he was invited, as were Dani, Tom, Frank, Francisco and Gloria (our landlords) but NOT George and Alyce! Tom and Frank brought along two other gay couples…not OUR type! John had a great time smashing the traditional piñata that the 'kids' bought for him. There was candy everywhere as he broke it open! After dinner we sat around the pool until we realized that it was around two-thirty in the morning. It was a great fiesta. John went home to bed while I walked our lady friend, Dani, home.

March 1st we headed out on our road trip to Chiapas and Oaxaca, which would take us to Tuxtla Gutierrez and San Cristobal de las Casas south of Mexico City, arriving two days later. While in Tuxtla, we visited Canon Del Sumidero, Chiapas Del Corzo and the Tuxtla Zoo, known as ZOOMAT. The next day we were in San Cristobal, 2163 meters above sea level. It was here that John lost his keys and remote starter for the vehicle alarm in the garage under the police station – a very memorable visit indeed! We had parked in the garage and walked around the town for about two hours. When it came time to go back to the car, the keys were not on his belt clip. We retraced our steps without success. Eventually, we would find a locksmith who could disarm the alarm. Using my key we were able to start the vehicle. We were concerned that we could no longer alarm the vehicle for the duration of our trip.

Early the next morning we headed south to Lagos Montebello near the Guatemalan border. The lakes there were idyllic. Unfortunately, because of high bacteria levels, they were unswimable. Except for that, they would have been great for skinny dipping! Almost like in Canada…

We changed our itinerary and headed back to Palenque and the ruins the next morning, stopping briefly at Agua Azul along the route to see the cascading waterfalls. Before touring Palenque the next day, we arranged to visit the royal tomb of Pakal, one of the great Mayan rulers, climbing down and then up the '69' steps. Rather auspicious for gay guys, don't you think? It is supposedly a good omen for those who are privileged to see it. It is the only royal tomb in North America. As of this writing, it is closed to visitors.

Leaving our hotel in Palenque at six in the morning, we headed to the ruins at Yaxchilan and Bonampak on an escorted tour. Honestly, with all of the rumors about the Zapatistas, I didn't want John to drive our vehicle there. Two hours into the trip, we stopped in the jungle to have a traditional Mayan breakfast cooked over an open fire. We boarded the van and headed south once again. We took a *lancha* (small boat) from Frontera to the ruins at Yaxchilan. Later in the day we toured Bonampak with its colored frescoes still intact from 800 A.D. The following morning we headed back on the eight hour drive to Progreso.

Mid-June saw us invited to Tom and Franks' beach condo, in a small town just west of Progreso. They were having a BBQ for some of their gay friends from the city. Up until that time, John and I had only been to public gatherings of gay guys – art exhibitions, restaurants, theaters, etc. In fact, we had never been to any of the city's gay bars (They did have three, in fact.) There were to be about ten couples attending, although we later found out that some were single. Some we had met from previous functions. In ages, they ranged from twenties to late sixties. The majority were Americans, but there were three or four Mexicans. We were the only Canadians.

We arrived after the BBQ in late afternoon, but there were still salads and snacks and drinks. We made our introductions and then proceeded to mingle. We had not previously met many of the guests. It was a sunny afternoon until the storm clouds rolled overhead...figuratively speaking...

As it got warmer we removed our shirts as had many of the other guys. Surprisingly, John was the only one with a nipple ring. This was of interest to many of the guys. "Did it hurt?" etc. One young guy, presumably Mexican, asked if he could touch it. John looked at me for approval. Not wanting to seem prudish or possessive, I agreed to let him do that. Then of course, he wanted to taste it...Go for it! We were all outside on the patio. What harm could come from it? And so he proceeded to put his mouth on John's nipple and tug at the ring with his teeth. Everyone seemed amused by his behavior and maybe just a little envious of him! And then it was over with and we all went back to chatting. John and I decided to go for a swim in the Gulf. We needed to cool off...things went downhill very quickly and we needed to leave.

When we drove back to Progreso we were both quiet. It wasn't until we reached home that we would discuss the day's events. Unlocking the door, I dissolved into tears and apologized to John for letting things get so totally out of hand. I felt that in some way I had encouraged it, starting with the episode with the nipple ring.

We didn't see Tom and Frank, or any of the others until after we came back from Canada the following fall, three months later. What must they have thought of us? Did they even know what had transpired that afternoon? I will leave this episode to your imagination...

Over the next few weeks we packed up our belongings and stored them for the summer. The casa was rented out for the summer to Mexicans who would pay the higher rent...five times what we were paying. We were headed north on a three month trek through Mexico, the southern United States and then to Canada to see John's and my children. On June 14th we picked up our *balls*, leaving Progreso behind...

***

Two days later we approached the outskirts of Mexico City – one of the largest cities in the world! We had discussed our options with Ross and he advised us to take a route northeast before we got into the actual city. We had well marked road maps (a must anywhere in Mexico). What we didn't count on was the absence of street signs. It is not uncommon in Mexico City for people to take down signs so the bill collectors cannot find them. If the street name is missing, the government will not replace them. GPS was out of the question in Mexico at that time.

At one point, we found ourselves in the city. Where were the suburbs? We were on a five lane highway which only went one way, with a boulevard in the middle. The traffic signals were not functioning, so John pulled to a stop, watched for oncoming cars and made a right turn. WRONG! We were immediately whistled over by a foot patrolman. In Spanish, as best we could understand, he explained that we had "disobeyed/disrespected" his fellow officer who was directing traffic on the far LEFT side of the highway. What officer? There were cars and people everywhere. The fine or "multa" for this particular offense was 2300 pesos...about $200 USD. We had the option of going to the police station to pay it OR we could pay on the spot. Who the hell could find the police station in the largest city in the world? We paid him cash and were allowed to drive off *without an actual ticket.* I was sure that his superiors would never see the money. He did however point us in the direction of the correct road to Queretaro, north of Mexico City – our destination for the night. Or so we thought...

An hour later we stopped a federal police officer to ask for more directions. I know...not a manly thing to do, but then again we are GAY men. His directions put us right back in Mexico City, lost again! Stopping at a Pemex gas station, we asked once again for directions. Perfecto!

Just when we got almost out of the city, a motorcycle policeman pulled us over to inspect our vehicle registration papers. We were driving legally with Canadian plates. In Mexico, when you enter the country with your vehicle you must get papers and a sticker from the customs allowing you to drive it while there. We had those. He took our papers, the Mexican registration papers, John's driver's license, his passport and our Mexican travel documents over to a nearby police car. When he returned he informed us that our documents were NOT in order. We had two options – leave the vehicle and accompany him to the police station OR pay another "multa". Here we go again.

There was no arguing right or wrong, although John certainly tried for over an hour in faltering Spanish. We weren't leaving our vehicle on the side street in Mexico City loaded with many of our possessions...horror stories. How did we know we would make it to a police station? We had no choice but to pay the outrageous fine. The original documents were securely tucked inside the officer's uniform jacket. This time the fine was 7600 pesos – about $700 USD!!!!! If we paid him, he would escort us out of Mexico City and guarantee us safe passage. Yeah, right?

There was one thing wrong with this option. We didn't have 7600 pesos on us. *"No problema, senores!"* There was a bank machine across the way. He rigged the traffic signals so we could cross. You can't get money out of dead tourists! He followed us to the machine. (You don't want tourists to get mugged outside a bank machine!) When we emerged, he motioned for us to follow him back across the street and give him the money once we were back in our vehicle. When we did, he returned all of the documents. As promised, we had a motorcycle escort out of Mexico City. It was like being raped and then having the rapist drive you home so you won't get raped again! We had been gang banged in

Mexico City…twice in one afternoon…by the police who were there to protect us from criminals.

As night fell, we reached our destination – Queretaro. I made John promise to stop at the first hotel/motel we came across. As luck would have it, it was one of Mexico's notorious "auto hotels" – found everywhere – hotels where people went for a few hours to have sex with another stranger, or in some cases, their spouses. Not much privacy in some Mexican homes, especially the traditional Mayan ones.

No amount of porn channels or overhead mirrors could induce us that night. We showered and went to bed, reliving the 'figurative rapes' until we finally fell asleep. We were still two days from the US border at Laredo, Texas. We had no more 'dinero' should we be stopped again. We would not have access to any more money until the first of July now two days away.

***

We crossed the US border at Nuevo Laredo and entered into Laredo, Texas. We sailed through the border, no more corrupt police to stop us, we hoped! We originally intended to head for Lake Charles, Louisiana where we knew a guy whom we had met on the beach in Progreso WITH his girlfriend! He wasn't gay, but he was cute. He was working out of town when we called him on his cell. Instead we stopped for the night in Columbia, Texas, south of Houston. Our vacation funds had taken a hit in Mexico City; nevertheless we celebrated being out of Mexico, with steak at a nearby restaurant next to the hotel...credit cards to the rescue!

We followed the Texas Independence Trail north to Huntsville, Texas where we set up camp in Sam Houston State Park. We had brought our tent so we could camp along the way. Short of funds now, it made great sense, even in the extreme heat of the Texan summer. We stopped for a few groceries before we set up camp.

In the morning, I cooked bacon and eggs on our camp stove. It was Fathers' Day, 2005. My daughters had no idea where we were at that point so I decided to telephone them. It was great to hear their voices. That night, John and I tried to sleep in our tent with the temperature hovering around ninety degrees at eleven o'clock at night! We were surrounded by fireflies when we looked out of the tent. It was an awesome sight. I had never seen so many in one place.

The following day, we headed north through Lufkin, Carthage, and Shreveport, arriving at Hope, Arkansas – home of former US President Bill Clinton. Since I am a political junkie, I had to see the place. When would I get the chance again, John? He caved into my request even though he is essentially non-political.

We left Hope behind (the town that is) and made our way east towards Memphis the next afternoon, continuing on to Cumberland State Park...more camping.

We detoured south the next morning, heading for Hiawassee State Park, near the Ocoee River, whitewater rafting site of the 1996 Atlanta Olympic Games. This truly was rafting country. When in Rome... The next morning we boarded our two man raft down the River – my first ever rafting experience. John had white watered in Canada with his ex-wife and sons. It was idyllic until we went aground on the rocks and had to get into the chilly waters to lift off the raft. *Blue balls...*

Further down stream we stopped for lunch on a little island. Going ashore, John took off his life jacket, heeding the call of Nature. We had a little something to eat and then reboarded the raft and headed downstream again. John realized too late that he had left his life vest on shore! There was no way that we could paddle upstream over the rocks. And we were not going to pay for another lifejacket! More *blue balls* after we paddled to the shore and got back into the cold water to walk upstream and across from the island. There was no safe shore as it was all brush. I was up to my nipples in water this time, stepping over submerged tree branches. Somehow we managed to get back and retrieve the jacket. The rest of the trip was uneventful.

That night, in the tranquility of the Tennessee woods, I wrote –

Tennessee Night

In the darkness
Of the Tennessee woods,
Fireflies illuminate the night.
Softly, a country western song
Plays across our campsite.

Occasionally, a flashlight
Searches the surrounding trees,
As the wind whispers through them.
The smell of campfires
Threads its' way
Between the breezes.

We are alone to the world.
You and I,
Each in our thoughts.
I can only but wonder
What yours might be,
But for me,
They are thoughts of a future,
Together.
Not by accident are we here,
Our minds contemplating
Tomorrow and tomorrows,
Rafting down the river of life,
Staying our course,
No matter how rough may be
The waters of our journey.

It was time to head north the next day, crossing the Cherohala Skyway into North Carolina. This connected to the famous Blue Ridge Parkway. Neither of us had traveled this route before. It was incredibly beautiful country, traveling through the mountains.

***

Two weeks after leaving Progreso, we arrived in Lansing, Michigan. Only the Detroit River now separated us from Canada. We had been away from Canada for several months and were anxious to cross the border. Once again we chose to spend the night at our friend's apartment. From there we could shop various stores and malls while he was at work during the day. At night, I prepared dinner for all of us, we watched some TV and then went to bed, as before, he in his bed, and John and I on the pullout couch as we had done before.

We had been introduced by Jack – John's former partner, in the spring of 2004. We all attended the same Church, which is where I met him one Sunday morning. When Jack and I were going our separate ways, he had thought that Ralph and I might hit it off. None of us was ever positive about Ralph's sexual preferences, in spite of two divorces. Maybe he truly was bisexual? He had a brief affair with John before I ever met him. He knew that we were definitely gay, but in reality we all felt that he was afraid to come out because of his children. I could relate to that. I was seriously attracted to him, but never crossed the line beyond friendship. When you truly care about someone's friendship, you are reticent to change the dynamics.

Before I left Canada to join John, I had gone out for dinner with Ralph. We met at a great Italian restaurant where we asked the chef to surprise us, while we drank some very good wine. In another time, another place, things might have been different. I respected him too much to ask personal questions, though I knew he had been more than 'just friends' with John. At the end of the evening I gave him a special paper weight – a gift of our friendship.

We had great times together – public times – Church, restaurants, bowling, theater, movies, etc. We were always in a group. It was strange staying at his apartment with John. I could not imagine what was going through his head when he saw John and me semi-naked together on his couch, while he slept alone in his bedroom that night. For that matter, what went through John's head? He had told me all about their brief relationship. We had no secrets. I trusted that John had told me everything about their relationship.

In our minds we all had boundaries. Friendship was too important to cross the line.

Ironic statement isn't that coming from me? Considering that was exactly what John and I had both done to Jack…There would be no way back, similar to what was going on between Jack and John. We left the US on June 30th, crossing the border into Canada. For the next two weeks we visited my family and friends in Windsor, before heading east to see John's family and friends and ultimately, his older son in Nova Scotia, just southeast of Halifax.

***

We had planned the trip north so that we could reconnect with our old friends. Some were friends of John's near Toronto. Others were new friends we had met in Mexico over the winter – the snowbirds. Our itinerary was to be Ontario, Quebec, New Brunswick and Nova Scotia, traveling via the shortest route through the USA.

By the time we returned to Progreso, we had planned on traveling over 20,000 kilometers – approximately 12,000 miles that summer.

Our first visit was near the Bruce Trail – Tobermory, Ontario, on Lake Huron. We had met a couple in Progreso the previous March. They had invited us to spend a couple of days at their cottage. These were also the people who owned the condo in old Montreal where we would be staying for a wedding in late August. We stayed longer than expected – it was so relaxing after the previous month of travel from Mexico.

We headed south to John's old hometown to see his former neighbors. He was pleasantly surprised that one of them had arranged a dinner party for us, inviting all of the other friends – people who had been friends of him and his ex-wife!

From there, we went northeast of Toronto to visit Jack's mother and his younger brother and his wife. I had previously met them in April when we had flown to Canada. They were wonderful people, inviting us to stay overnight at their place. They obviously harbored no animosity towards John or me. We actually stayed for three nights. John had not been feeling well; he had a persistent cough. He had also developed a sore tooth. Most nights we cooked dinner for them since they were both working. One evening we all went out to dinner. There was this great Brazilian waiter…yes, he was gay. Hard to say what was better, the food or the thought about the waiter!

When John finally felt better, we headed for his boyhood town northeast of Toronto, Ontario. His cousins all lived there. His parents were buried there behind the rural church. We walked through the cemetery with him pointing out the headstones of his parents, where he stopped while I walked away to give him some privacy, and then he identified the headstones of departed relatives. I wondered what he might have said to his parents. In my recent journey, I had visited the grave of my father and taken out a crayon and made a 'rubbing' of his name. I carried it in my wallet, along with a laminated photo of him.

I had met the cousins previously when we stayed over on our way to camping in September 2004. While in the area we had lunch with John's ex-wife's mother and her sister! That was interesting. They couldn't have been nicer...of course; we brought her flowers...what woman doesn't like flowers and candy at the age of eighty-three?

John's tooth finally got the better of him. I was prepared to cancel the trip to Nova Scotia if he didn't get it treated. We made an emergency visit to the dentist – ouch! He recommended a root canal! Now was not the time. We were headed east to the Maritimes for at least ten days. Painkillers would delay the needed surgery we hoped. Later that night we pitched our tent beside the Thousand Islands National Park in Brockville, on Lake Ontario

The next morning, we crossed back into the US on our way to New Brunswick. This was really the shortest route, traveling through New York,

Vermont, New Hampshire and Maine. After three days we reached the New Brunswick/Maine border at St. Stephen's. We had met two other friends who lived on an island not far from near there back in Progreso. They were actually a lesbian couple with whom we had spent a fair amount of time in Mexico while they were there the previous winter. Our plan was to spend a few days at their cottage and then head to Nova Scotia via the ferry service. That night we received a frantic call from John's older son asking us to come to Nova Scotia the next morning. As the sun rose, we left the island and headed to the ferry in Saint John. The Bay of Fundy was very cold for a summer day. The seas were choppy. We both felt queasy. We landed at Digby, NS. Late in the afternoon, we arrived at his son's place near Halifax. We still had a three hour drive north to his son's girlfriends' house. With John and his son in the front seat, and me and his son's dog in the back, we drove northeast. It had been a very long day by the time we got there. We fell asleep in sleeping bags on the family room floor in each other's arms – not too tired for a little recreation while his son and girlfriend were sleeping in the next room!

We spent seven days in Nova Scotia with John's son and his girlfriend's family. During that time we visited Halifax, New Glasgow, Annapolis and Port Royal, as well as Fort Ste. Anne.

All of our waking hours were with them. The only alone time we had was at night in bed. We managed to enjoy these private moments while rehashing the day's events. Returning to Halifax, we took his son shopping for much needed work clothes at a second-hand store. We spent the last night in Nova Scotia at the cottage where the boys lived while they worked in the area chopping trees. John and I prepared the dinner.

On our last morning in Nova Scotia, shortly after breakfast, we received an urgent message from my former wife on John's cell phone. My eighty-three year old mother had been hospitalized. I was needed back home in Ontario.

***

We left Nova Scotia at 9:00 a.m. on August 3rd, arriving in Windsor, my hometown, at 11:45 p.m. August 4th, with an overnight stop in Hampton Beach, New Hampshire. The fastest route was utilizing the Massachusetts and New York Turnpikes. While we were on our way my wife had telephoned asking us to spend the night at HER place – my old house. Now *that* was a dilemma. Should we or not? I decided that she would not have asked if she wasn't comfortable with it, so I accepted her generous offer with John's approval.

When we arrived near midnight, she offered us snacks and a glass of wine. We sat outside on HER patio and talked before heading to bed. It was indeed strange to be there, not just because she was in the next room. John and I were sleeping in the same bed where my wife had caught me with 'the other man' almost one and a half years before! As it had been at our friend's in Michigan, I wondered what must be going through her mind. I know what was going through mine. There had been other men with me in that bed previously. Actually, 'the other man' had been back once more. Albeit reluctantly. There was another young teacher, a blue-collar worker, and another older guy I'd rather forget! Respectfully, I never invited guys into the bedroom which I shared with my wife.

I visited the hospital the next morning. My mother was stable and cognizant of my presence. Awaiting her test results, we discussed her options. She did not have the option of returning to her apartment. Her *balls* would land in a nursing home – no question. After a few days, the results came back – inoperable pancreatic cancer. It was terminal. How soon could not be said. Realizing her fate, she agreed to sign the necessary papers for transfer to a long term care facility…a euphemism for a place to die. She rallied after doing that, with the help of the narcotics no doubt. Her nurses were awesome (inappropriately, I must admit that her one male nurse was quite handsome…) I spent two nights at her bedside and she began to show signs of improvement.

On the Thursday, assured of her stability by her doctors, John and I drove to Montreal for the wedding of one of his teacher friends, who was marrying my Spanish teacher from Progreso. We were using our friends' condo. The location was great – about six blocks from Montreal's gay village - St. Catherine's Street.

Of course, we strolled through the village noticing all of the men walking hand in hand that night. Unlike Toronto's Church Street, St. Catherine's Street was a cultural Mecca for straight and gay people. There were many restaurants catering to both groups. Not visible were the gay only bars and spas which were prevalent in Toronto. It was comfortable to be with John...and there were many hot guys too. The restaurant where we ate was filled with gay men of all ages. We could walk down the street holding hands!

Early the next morning, I received another call from my wife – my mother had gone into a coma. John arranged for the next plane home for me while I packed and headed to the airport at Dorval, leaving him to attend the wedding alone. While waiting for my boarding call, I wrote –

One Final Goodbye

Alone in the airport
I awaited my boarding call
Taking me home to you,
One last time –
One final goodbye.

Where had the years gone?
Only yesterday
I played in the fields of corn and tomatoes,
Raced around the ball diamonds,
Skinned knees and elbows,
On my way
To premature manhood,
Even before
You taught me to drive a car –
Two-footed.

I waited and watched

As you picked up the pieces of your life,
Hopeful
That you would once again
Or maybe for the first time,
Find happiness –
Ever illusive.
Except for brief periods of time,
It came and went, then came and went again,
Before darkness fell.

Deprived of sight,
You struggled to survive – alone
In a world made only of shadows,
Growing dimmer day by day,
And then, mercifully,
God heard your prayers
And released your soul
From its earthly ties,
But not before –
One last goodbye.

Three days later she was gone! The last night, my
two daughters and I joined hands with her, said a
prayer (so unlike the old me) and told her that
she could go. One last goodbye…an hour later
the male nurse called – her suffering had been
short lived. Mercifully the cancer had only been
diagnosed two weeks before – time enough for
my family to prepare for the eventuality.

Two days later I presided over the graveside
internment of her ashes with my immediate
family in attendance – my older sister and her
husband, my former wife, my two daughters,
their husbands and children, and John and I. I
read the poem which I had written in Montreal

and played one of her favorite hymns *"Beyond the Sunset"*. We had two weeks to get her affairs in order before heading back to Mexico. With the help of my daughters and ex-wife and John, we cleaned out her apartment, put the affairs in order and finished our business dealings and doctors' appointments. Mom had timed this well!

Before leaving we spent another night on our friend's couch in Michigan. Just after Labor Day, the trek home began – Indiana, Illinois, Iowa, Missouri – stopping to visit Jack for two days. We had a good friendly visit this time, unlike the last.

Heading south, we drove through Oklahoma and then Texas, stopping in Dallas. The next night we stopped again in San Antonio – my favorite city in the US – rather romantic cruising down the river at night. On September 13th we crossed the border at Laredo, Texas into Mexico. Heading south once again, we drove through Monterrey, Queretaro and San Juan Del Rio. We wanted to avoid Mexico City. From San Juan we headed to Puebla and then Cordoba. Four days later we were back at home in Progreso.

***

There was a lot to be done in the next month. Two women from Canada were renting our casa while they put the finishing touches to a college textbook they were writing. It sounded boring to me, but I guess they thought if they had to write, a beach in Mexico was the place to be. One of them was a friend of the lesbian couple we knew from New Brunswick. While they wrote, John and I were heading off on a three week bus trip north to the Barrancas Del Cobre near Chihuahua – the so-called Copper Canyon.

We had the whole house rewired before we left for Canada in June. The fluorescent tubes were all gone! Home Depot loved us – new lighting fixtures, remote controlled fans, etc.

That first Sunday we had breakfast around the corner at the hotel. Our friend's divorce was still pending and had now started to get downright nasty – name calling, threats, etc. He was still upbeat, although he had come to refer to his ex-wife as "The Shining" from the Stephen King novel of the same title. Bitterness was creeping in…his body was starting to show the effects of too much alcohol and probably too much womanizing!

As was our usual practice when at home in Progreso, we attended church every Sunday via live streaming on the Internet. It was broadcast from our home church in Michigan. Besides the music and the message, it was comforting to see our friends as the cameras panned the congregation. We invariably waved at them although they couldn't really see us.

The next week, John installed the new kitchen shelving which we had brought from Canada, and we went shopping for a new refrigerator – ours was too small for our weekly shopping – so un-Mexican. We avoided the town 'mercado'. We ended up buying a new stove as well – one that actually had a temperature control and a broiler. Next on our list of to-dos were new window coverings. We agreed on NO florals – not manly! We settled on wooden shutters for our bedroom to afford maximum privacy.

***

After John's birthday, we had continued to see our Canadian lady friend, Dani, and her teenage sons. When we went shopping into the city, we either took her or called to get a list of what she needed. Since she had no car in Mexico, she used public transit. Feeding two teenage boys required more groceries than could be brought home on a bus or found at a corner store in Progreso. We often shopped at a big box store and divided up the things between us.

Our friend worked odd jobs to help support herself and the boys. Besides the volunteer work at the library, she house-sat for different people in and around the town when they had to go north. Once in a while she 'hosted' at local restaurants – her job was to invite the tourists from the cruise ships into the restaurant. She spoke English, French and a little Spanish so she was a natural to invite the cruise ship passengers into the restaurants. She hated the work and soon quit.

Her boys kept her very busy – trying to keep them in check with an absentee father. She had raised her two boys to be fairly strict vegetarians – the oldest was no problem. The youngest developed a penchant for junk food, which she refused to support in their home. Having raised two teenage daughters, I was very familiar with a rebellious one! He rang all of her bells as often as he could. This probably explained why she so readily accepted any invitations to get out of the house. Since we were not bar types, we rarely saw her in any of the local places. She did let us know that she went out from time to time, but just socially. She had many girlfriends, both in Progreso and in the nearby city.

When we left for Canada in the summer, she stayed in Progreso with her boys. They had a two bedroom apartment over a restaurant which overlooked the Gulf.

At the end of September, she invited us to a local bar to see a drag show. While we were in Canada, her long lost husband had finally arrived in Mexico. John had met him previously. He was a tall, handsome man with graying hair. When we met him, he gave us both a big hug and a kiss on the cheek. Curious? Could he be bisexual? After that, he always greeted us the same way. No qualms about anyone seeing him do that...

What had he really been up to in the Far East while our friend and her boys were in Mexico? If he had been my husband, I would have made him take an HIV/STD test...a girl can't be too careful. There were lots of bisexual men in Mexico – married men. They looked macho, had wives or mistresses, but they still liked sex with other men.

The drag show was great – five Mexican guys with makeup, women's clothing and high heels, lip syncing to Mexican and American music. The hit of the show was 'Cher' – okay, not *the* Cher.

Lip synching a medley of Cher songs in English, he/she came out in an all white outfit with a lacy cape. Under the cape was a white jump suit – actually ribbons of fabric constructed like a lattice work with lots of skin showing. We all wondered how in the world he hid his 'equipment'. He was totally shaved and there was bare skin showing in his crotch, but no signs of a penis or *balls.* Ouch! I was later to learn how important Duct tape is to such performers...

***

One night, the wind had come up and it started to rain. We awoke about 4 a.m. to a flapping screen door on the south side of the house. We both thought we had locked that one. We always left it locked and the inner door open and unlocked for fresh air. When John got up to check on it, we had been robbed!

Gone was his laptop computer, his wallet which he had left on the dining room table, and his cell phone. Of course, his wallet contained his driver's license, credit cards, bank cards and a few other items. There was also four thousand pesos in cash! The thief had entered through a side window while we were asleep not twenty feet away in our bedroom. What if we had awakened? I was devastated...On the computer we had just uploaded all of our photos from the summer trip to Canada. We had erased the cards and had not made a backup. Life has a way of teaching us valuable lessons, doesn't it? We'd been kicked in the *balls* again!

I was the more upset I guess, and nothing of mine had even been stolen. What if he came back? Whoever it was now knew what else we had in the house. John didn't appear to be concerned, but I certainly was! What would we tell the women who were coming to stay at our place in two weeks? Should we tell them?

We promptly arranged for *protectores* (steel grates) to be installed on the windows.

Our landlord was so ashamed that one of his countrymen would do this to foreigners. He went directly to the police and protested. Several weeks later a young man was brought to our house by the police. He admitted the break-in. All of the stolen items were long gone. As it turned out, he also admitted to breaking into several Mexican homes!

***

Our Canadian guests arrived in late October. They seemed like nice ladies, forty-ish. We weren't sure that we would tell them about the robbery on their first day with us. John waited for an opportune time. Two days before we left, he told them. They were cool; they would make sure that all doors and windows were locked at night and when they went out. Francisco, our landlord, would watch over them.

On October 29th we boarded the first of many buses and began our three week trip to the Copper Canyon (Los Barrancas del Cobre) and northern Mexico. Three buses and a subway ride later, through the heart of Mexico City, we arrived in Toluca, west of Mexico City. We had been on the bus for twenty-four hours! We were exhausted, checking into a hotel right in the bus terminal. Coincidentally, it was called *Hotel Terminal.* Where was Stephen King? After a light supper we headed back to our room.

We had no sooner arrived in the room then John went into convulsions. He started to get chills and a fever. I wrapped him in all of the blankets I could find. He continued to convulse. I had never seen him like that before. He managed to tell me that this happened a couple of times before I met him. He eventually did calm down, but I spent the night watching his every breath! By morning he was back to normal, thank God! It had not been an auspicious start. What if he got ill again…thousands of miles from Progreso? My Spanish was still very limited.

After breakfast we boarded another bus to Guadalajara – eight hours away. We knew that Guadalajara was the center of gay activity in Mexico. We had chatted online with a couple of guys there in the months before the trip. We had dinner at the historical center, surrounded by the beautiful old buildings, and man watched. There were some great looking guys, including our waiter. If only we had the nerve? Maybe room service to our hotel?

We still had two more days of bus trips before we reached Los Mochis on the western coast of Mexico. We were planning on riding the train into the Canyon – 390 miles from Los Mochis. It was rated as THE best train ride in the world! In total it is 553 miles from one end to the other in Chihuahua. We were not disappointed, as it was first class and air-conditioned. Then again, it was definitely NOT Canadian first class! The vistas were incredible as the train – CHEPE – crossed thirty-six bridges and passed through eighty-seven tunnels.

We had reserved seats, but spent most of the time standing outside the bar car snapping photographs. The vistas were awesome- starting in the plains where we passed sesame and corn fields and cattle farms, fruit orchards, etc. As we began to ascend into the mountains, the train slowed. The peaks were spectacular. In the valleys were dry river beds. This was the dry season. There were just a few brief stops along the way where we dropped off food and farm goods. The Barrancas are very poorly populated. After seven hours we arrived at our destination – *Hotel Mansion Tarahumara* at El Divisadero, halfway point on the train to Chihuahua.

As we approached, it looked like a fairy tale castle made of limestone, with bright red tile turrets – very German looking. Circling it were forty cabins of rustic stone and cedar construction, built into the rock. The view from the terrace of the main building was breath-taking to say the least. Hummingbirds flittered around the many feeders.

On the train from El Fuerte we had met another couple who, coincidentally, were staying at the *Mansion*. They were from Pennsylvania. As it turned out, our cabins were side by side. From the beginning we had hit it off. They had no problem with gay guys. We had no problem with straight people. While other guests came and went during the week, we were the only ones staying for the full week.

Our first dinner involved only twelve people. The Mansion was not busy in November. For the next six days we ate all of our meals with the other couple and whoever happened to be there. We hiked during the day, up and down the mountain sides, taking picnic lunches prepared for us by the kitchen staff. Looking back, I wonder why we never thought of hiking alone and enjoying some romantic moments in one of the thousand secluded spots among the trees...

The four of us took side trips to the nearby towns and to a Tarahumara village, which did not seem part of the twenty-first century, or the twentieth for that matter. The homes were built in caves, with roofs blackened by cooking fires. All of their possessions were on display...no doors, no closets and no electrical appliances of any nature. Bathrooms were non-existent. Their animals lived with them! Others lived in small thatched huts and a few actually had a framed house. There was a wide diversity on the Reserve.

On a few occasions, we used the hotel's pool and Jacuzzi. Neither was warm enough for us, even though indoors. The temperature at eight thousand feet was quite cool. Running from the pool to our cabin was the norm after swimming. We learned to run fast!

Along with our new friends, we hiked various trails, following the horse and donkey 'droppings'. Actually we got lost the first time. On the second hike, we took along a picnic lunch from the hotel. Alas, there were no tidbits to drop along the way to mark our way back should we become lost again. Fortunately, we didn't.

Breakfasts and dinners were always a new experience. The first night there were Americans, Mexicans and Germans. Most of the Mexicans spoke some English. Neither of our friends nor did I speak much Spanish, so John was able to translate if needed. Amongst those we met were two environmentalists from California, a Mexican mother and her teenage son who was training to be a chef, another young Mexican medical student and his nutritionist wife, two other Californians, presumed to be gay, who were film makers of a sort...not porn as far as we understood! One or two nights there were RV-ers – a caravan who had put their RVs on the flatcars for the travel across the mountains. Where else but in Mexico could you put your RV on a train and then sit outside on the same flatcar in your lawn chairs, drinking beer and maybe have a BBQ? Of course, the RV-ers had their own security guards to watch over their units while they were parked in a siding for the night. Quite the life! Almost gypsy-like.

Friday came and we decided to leave for Chihuahua with our new friends. And so began the fifty-two hour bus trip back to Progreso via Chihuahua, Zacatecas, Guanajuato and Mexico City.

Zacatecas and Guanajuato are both UNESCO World Heritage Cities. Zacatecas was designated because of its architecture. It also boasts a cable car ride from the top of the mountain, 'La Bufa' and an old silver mine beneath the city, 'El Eden', which has been restored as a tourist attraction, complete with a very contemporary disco five stories below ground. Another interesting site was the oldest bullring in Mexico, which had been converted into a first class hotel – the *Quinta Real.*

Guanajuato is an amazing city – literally. They have transformed the old underground sewers and aqueducts into roadways with a series of tunnels through the mountain on which it is built. The waters were diverted many years ago into a dammed lake. There are very few above ground streets. It truly was amazing how the people got around without getting lost.

We headed for Mexico City the next morning. We got off the bus at the Terminal Norte and boarded the subway again. At the eastern terminal – TAPO - we boarded another bus for Cordoba, east of Puebla. After spending the night, we started on our final bus ride!

We returned to our casa three weeks after we had left.

Our renters were safe and sound. We spent their last three days entertaining them and touring nearby ruins. After they flew back to Canada, we went to the sixty-fifth birthday party of a Mexican friend whom we had met in June before we left for Canada. We had had dinner with him and his partner at our place in Progreso, and had been to their place in the nearby city for dinner and drinks. We enjoyed their company...more social friends!

***

It was fast approaching Christmas...actually our first Christmas alone together in Mexico. We were expecting guests from Canada on Boxing Day and then another from Detroit, Christina, right after New Year's. The former were a lesbian couple from New Brunswick whom we had met the year before and then visited in Canada in the summer. The latter was a woman minister friend who we had come to know at our church in Detroit.

Before any company would arrive, we wanted to paint throughout the house. It was an ugly mushroom color...blah. This was going to be a challenge – combining our personal color biases. Amazingly we agreed on the colors – yellow, green and tomato red...all the colors present in the pre-existing tiles in the kitchen (ugly as they were). Eleven gallons of paint later we finished. Endless hours of rolling, brushing and then cleaning up and re-arranging the furniture. It certainly tested our patience with each other.

Halfway through the process my children and grandchildren arrived in Cozumel on a Royal Caribbean cruise. We stopped work for two days and went to spend their only day in port – a pre-Christmas – since we wouldn't be together on the twenty-fifth this year…the first time in their lifetimes!

It was a bittersweet day – only eight hours to spend together. I wanted to spend a few hours alone with the four grand kids. We planned on going to a nature reserve, only to discover that it had been destroyed by Hurricane Wilma in October. The only available place was a small maritime museum. They were all too young to enjoy the displays. Oh well…there was always shopping at the dollar stores. John held on to two and I held on to the other two. Thank God for those dollar stores!

We all met up for lunch at a local spot – *Fat Tuesdays*, lots of margaritas. Later, my two sons-in-law and John went snorkeling in the Caribbean waters. I thought it was a good idea for John to be alone with them. Let them get to know him better. It also gave me time alone with my daughters and their children. We walked and shopped and then walked and shopped some more. While frolicking in the sea with my son-in-law, John lost his commitment ring in the waves… ominous?

Too soon, the guys returned from snorkeling. They had to be on board their ship, *Legend of the Seas*, by five o'clock. Fortunately, their launch left from the same dock in Cozumel as did our ferry back to Playa Del Carmen. They went to the left as we headed right…

In my mind were visions of parents and children being separated during World War II – being sent off to concentration camps? I felt that my granddaughters were being pulled away from me. Literally, pulled out of my arms. Extreme? Overly dramatic? We were all very emotional, including my two daughters. We didn't know when we would see each other again, except via web cam. I was disconsolate as our ferry passed by the enormous cruise ship which would take them back to the US and home to Canada for a real northern Christmas...carols, snow, Santa Claus, Christmas trees, etc.

John and I got off the ferry, running through the rain, which masked my tears, and caught the next bus back to Progreso. Four hours of reflection of the day's events...recalling their tearful faces.

Painting completed, we put up a token Christmas tree complete with fiber optic lights. We spent Christmas Eve (*Noche Buena*) with our Mexican family. It was difficult for me. John hadn't spent much time with his sons after the divorce. Christmas was not a family occasion for him. In reality, I had never enjoyed Christmas as a result of my own father's decision when I was a child, to take his mother to Florida! Christmas equated with abandonment issues, which were compounded when my parents ultimately divorced two years later.

***

Christmas Eve – *Noche Buena* in Mexico – lasted until four o'clock in the morning! We drank and danced and ate in the portico outside our casa, decorated with real Mexican poinsettias, three winter piñatas and colorful lights, strung between the columns of the carport. Shortly after midnight the presents appeared. Unlike Canadian or American Christmases, Mexicans tend to be very practical in their gift giving. We had purchased presents for each member of Francisco's family. They had done the same for us. None of the gifts was extravagant! They consisted of earrings, polo shirts, scarves, shirts and blouses. Unusual by American standards, no gift certificates and no gift cards! We were rather surprised when Tomas, Francisco's son, gave him a pair of bikini underwear styled like an elephant mask, complete with the appropriate holder for his 'trunk'...We could never have imagined giving that to our respective fathers, let alone receive a pair from one of our children!

Around four o'clock in the morning we cleaned up and headed for bed...no visions of sugar plums. In the morning, when we finally awoke, John and I exchanged simple gifts. I gave him a Spanish version of Dan Brown's *Angels and Demons*. He gave me a beautiful leather sculpture done by a local French expatriate. Christmas dinner was spent at a house on the beach which had been rented for three months by a couple from Western Canada whom we knew them from the last year when they were in Progreso and attended John's birthday fiesta at the hotel with the gang. At the moment, they were the only snowbirds who had arrived from the north. We skipped the turkey and cranberries, instead eating fresh fish and sweet potatoes and Brussels sprouts....very non-traditional...

We did spend the early part of New Year's Eve with them at their beach house. Bobbi had prepared appetizers for about twelve of us - Canadians, Americans, Mexicans and a couple originally from East Germany who was now living outside of Detroit, Michigan. The husband's mother, a journalist, was there from her home in Spain. The latter three had originally come to Progreso to stay at a condo across the street. Our Canadian friends weren't planning on being awake at midnight. They always went to bed at nine o'clock. With the combination of loud music, lame jokes and the poor acoustics in their place, John and I left at nine and headed to another friend's place to welcome the New Year with them and a few of their friends. We stood on the balcony at midnight singing Auld Lang Syne while overlooking the quiet waters of the Gulf of Mexico.

***

John took another teaching job shortly thereafter – two hours per day, teaching French to two thirty-something Mexicans, a married couple from Veracruz. We had often talked about him going back to some teaching. He enjoyed it. As for me, I was apprehensive. What would I do while he was at work? I didn't want to teach again. I could only cook and clean so much. I wasn't a regular beach walker. Volunteering was out! I didn't speak Spanish...

When my wife and I were still together, and when she was at work, I played on the Internet chat lines. Before I knew it, I was there the whole time that she was away. I was out of control – chatting online with other men, and sometimes meeting them. I did not want to get on that treadmill again!

The only thing I enjoyed doing was my writing. I had written and published one book the previous year about my coming out. It came about as a result of the journal I had begun to write in the hospital after the threatened suicide attempt in 2005. As I was 'coming out' I realized that there were few books written by older men like me coping with this process. The result was "Not My Father's Footsteps", published in the US under the pseudonym of Bryan Dean. Since then, I had written a manuscript, the sequel, entitled *"Don't Look Back"* along with over seventy original poems. The proposed title of the poetry anthology was *In Spirit's Time – An Anthology of Emotions.* From all accounts, I was good at writing. I mulled over writing a history of …too much research in Spanish, even though our landlord was a virtual font of knowledge about the town. Bad idea.

I had just finished reading two fictional accounts of gay men which took place in Providence, Rhode Island, in the Northeastern United States. The author had interwoven their stories, as they interacted one summer. It was one of those light bulb moments!!!!!!!!!!!!!!

I could write a fictional account involving the various snowbirds with whom we had come in contact with since we arrived.

I would call it *"Balls!"* the theme of a talk I had heard our Minister give when we were back in Canada.

***

John and I kept rolling along – peaks and valleys presented themselves in our relationship. By late March and early April all of the snowbirds had flown north again. Just prior to their leaving, we held a BBQ, attended by the last of the flock...a real Canadian BBQ with burgers, potato salad, baked beans, etc. About thirty people came. After lunch we all headed to the local watering hole to watch the regular Saturday afternoon drag show. Yes, Progreso still had a real drag show. John had previously arranged for 'Cher' to be among the performers. None of us were happy as we brought to a close the winter season. We would miss them all.

With John at school, the lure of the chat rooms persisted, but I tried to concentrate on my new novel. As long as I was writing, I was content. I didn't really look forward to finishing the book. Then what? But then, sooner than anticipated, the first draft of the manuscript was finished...so I thought. To further occupy my time, I signed up for Spanish classes with our woman friend. We attended classes two days a week for one and a half hours with a thirty-ish Mexican single guy who was our teacher.

When I wasn't in school, I would sometimes chat with one or two guys for a while in the morning. One was an older single guy from my hometown in Canada. I did not previously know him. The other guy was from Ohio, married, out to his wife, but not his two teenage children. There was not a chance that we would ever meet. That was not what I wanted. I just needed to talk with someone. I was lonesome when John wasn't around. I loved him too much to actually play behind his back. I became sensitive about his rejections of my many advances. Indeed, I was stressing him out….almost as much as myself.

One afternoon we had a BBQ with my Spanish teacher and another friend. A local restaurant owner, whom we had come to know, came to join us. After eating, the four of them got into a conversation about spirituality. I was never very good at debating and more or less sat there listening to all of the others. It didn't help that they were speaking in Spanish! John was so much more eloquent when he spoke, at least in English. His knowledge of spiritual matters far exceeded mine. I felt inadequate by comparison, not being able to interject any valid or pertinent comments. What was I doing with John? He and Jack were 'on par' when they had spiritual discussions. They both had a better understanding of the subject. I was a spiritual novice.

One night, shortly thereafter, as we were lying in bed, I felt overwhelmed by the events of the past few weeks. I had been 'simmering' for a variety of reasons – loneliness, lack of attention, missing my grandkids in Canada, feeling inadequate as his partner. Amidst tears, I blurted out, "I am leaving you, John!"

What transpired was a very serious talk -

Was there another man? NO!
Where would I go? I don't know…not back to Canada!
When would I go? I don't know…

The truth was that I didn't have any plans at the moment; I just needed him to know what I was feeling at the moment!

We discussed my feeling inadequate as his partner on a daily basis. He had different standards than me. John strove for perfection whenever he did something around the house. I was satisfied with mediocre. Sometimes I felt that I didn't cook right; I didn't iron his clothes properly; I irritated him when I would tidy up his stuff; I didn't rinse the dishes enough…and worst of all – his mother did it differently! She had been gone for many years now; he had been married for twenty-seven years before the divorce. Did his ex-wife experience the *"…not like my mother…"* comparisons too?

I loved him but deep down I felt that I couldn't meet his expectations of a partner. Bottom line…we were indeed complementary as I always said. At that moment it seemed to me like we were both on the same highway, alright, but each were in separate lanes that didn't always converge.

Neither of us slept well that night, but in the morning the sun came up again! Unsaid was that we needed to keep working through this. Over the next few weeks we carried on. John went off to school each day, while I continued to chat, write and do household chores when I wasn't taking my Spanish class.

***

Summer was upon us – our first full summer in Mexico. We had prepared for the heat, having installed air conditioning back in March in exchange for a month's rent.

Traditionally, Progreso was a mecca for the residents of the nearby city, whose temperatures were always ten degrees warmer. The town's population would swell during July and August. Traffic along the Malecón would crawl most evenings. Late at night, the place would swarm with young Mexicans cruising the beach...not unlike an American or Canadian resort town in the summer. Of course, there were occasional gay couples!

John and I finally got started on the exterior painting of our casa, which turned into a much bigger job than we had intended. Where were those hunky Latino guys when you needed them? Before we finished, we would be painting not only our place, but also the adjoining home of our landlord. When we finished, it resembled a grand hacienda. Our landlord's family would sit across the street admiring it.

A week later, we went to our first opera, seeing *Rigoletto* with our hotel owner friend and his Mexican wife.

That same week, our Dani, our Canadian friend became very ill and had to be hospitalized for five days. What she had presumed was a kidney infection turned out to be salmonella, accompanied by gastritis and anemia. Her resistance was very low. Initially she had a severe reaction to the prescribed medications. In the midst of this we were supposed to be celebrating her forty-second birthday! We had planned a taco bar with about twenty-five friends. Secretly, her husband had sent out all of the invitations by email. She was now in no condition for a party at this point. We were forced to cancel it until she could get back on her feet.

Looking for something more constructive to do in our spare time, we decided to expand the front terrace. We had talked with our friend Ross, who no longer owned the hotel around the corner. He arranged for one of his men to undertake the job. The upside was that we got to see him each day for ten days when he came by for coffee and to oversee the work. Neither of us had lost the desire to spend time with him. He still 'cranked our tractor' as a southern friend used to say!

In real time, we continued to work around the house. John changed some outdoor lighting fixtures. When that was done we began the task of painting our landlord's house – inside this time. We had previously talked about it. When they decided to go away for a week to the Caribbean coast, near Chetumal, we got into high gear. Confidently, his wife had told us to choose the colors. What had been purple and watermelon became a soft green and peach. The house was transformed. We eagerly awaited their return. Would they like it? Would they like what two gay guys had done to their home....kinda like *Queer Eye for the Straight Mexican Couple.*

***

Once we had completed all of the painting, we began making plans for a trip to Italy. Originally it was to have been Spain so we could practice our Spanish, but it turned out to be cheaper to go to Italy. Neither John nor I had ever been there, although John had spent time in Europe with his ex-wife when they were still married.

Our European tour was to begin in Italy on November 5, 2006 – one day before the US mid-term elections. I had never been to Europe before, although both of my daughters had during their teenage years. I was excited about it. I was also anxious about spending a whole month in one country.

The previous two weeks had been very hectic for us, as our landlord's oldest daughter got married in the main cathedral in the city. As her pseudo *tios* (uncles) we were invited, of course. Besides making travel plans, we were involved in pre-wedding festivities with her family. As family members arrived from the US, there were many social gatherings. We were expected to attend them all, dropping whatever we had planned on sometimes short notice. Mexicans are not known for planning ahead. Often times, the festivities didn't start until 11:00 pm and sometimes continued on 'til 3 or 4 am! When we did leave a party early, the music continued in the courtyard just outside our bedroom window. We reverted to using ear plugs on occasion in order to get some sleep. The lack of sleep, the parties and the daily efforts to finalize our travel plans did cause me some stressful moments. I came close to getting into arguments with John over minor things on several occasions.

I had wisely told him that we would each plan one half of the trip. I was responsible for Milan, Venice, Florence and Tuscany. He was responsible for Rome, Naples, Sorrento and the Amalfi Coast. We poured over the respective guidebooks, planning itineraries in each city and checking out accommodations. We both made extensive use of the Internet for information and bookings in each city.

A German friend had introduced us to *Gaydar* - an Internet site where gay men could hook up for accommodations, sex, dinner, etc. We found an American working in Milan and started to chat with him regularly. As it turned out, he was born and raised in the US – Michigan, specifically, just across the border from where I had lived in Canada. Talk about your small world!

In the Florence chat room, we chatted with a thirty-eight year old guy who was willing to rent us his house for a week. In Rome, we met another Italian guy in his early 40's who wanted to get together with the two of us for drinks or dinner.

John and I were both involved in checking out guys in the various cities we were going to be visiting. Besides Milan, Venice, Florence, and Rome, we were to spend some time in Siena and

Sorrento. The Internet site exposed us to lots of men all over Italy. Some appealed to us. Some did not. Several times a day we would check the site to see who was online and who had been checking us out.

Two days before the wedding, the bride and groom arrived from Playa Del Carmen. In fact, they had been married there in June in a civil wedding on the beach. This was to be THE church wedding. Because our landlord's home was filled with relatives, the bride and groom slept at our place each night before the wedding day.

On the day of the wedding we continued to research our trip until late in the afternoon when we started to get ready for the candlelight service in the cathedral.

The wedding dress had been stored at our home and the anxious bride decided that our place was the best place for her to get ready. When her 'dresser' failed to show up, her "tios" stepped in to help her. It brought back memories of my own daughters' weddings years earlier. While I was snapping pictures, I was brought to tears with the memories of those previous weddings. We persevered and she was soon ready for the limo ride into the city. After we saw her off, we headed out as well. It turned out to be a beautiful day. We left the reception at a nearby hacienda at about three o'clock in the morning!

Several of the out of town visitors stayed over for a few more days. The little get togethers continued. I was growing tired of this social whirl. Honestly, I had never been a party person, unlike John. Part of the problem with these parties, was that my Spanish was not yet adequate enough to follow the conversations amongst the family members. John, on the other hand, was comfortable at all times.

One night, after another family gathering, we came home. John got ready for bed. I powered on the computer to see what was happening on the *Gaydar* site. John became upset. He let me know in no uncertain terms that if I wanted to spend time with other guys that I should do so! That wasn't my intention! When I get frustrated, the Internet is a distraction.

For the next two and a half hours, after I had told him that I was going for a walk – alone, we discussed the 'problem'. With all of the activities surrounding the wedding, I was feeling isolated – unable to communicate with our Mexican family, most of whom spoke little English. Whenever we went out, I felt like the proverbial 'bump on the log". I wanted contact with other English speaking people. I needed someone to whom I could talk about John and my relationship. All of this was made worse by our being together 24/7 for most of the last two years! With all of our time spent planning the trip, and with John constantly looking over my shoulder to see what I was doing, I hadn't had any real conversation with anyone for the better part of a week. We eventually headed off to bed, each hugging our respective pillows. I hoped that what I tried to explain made sense to John. I did love him. I needed him to understand where I was coming from. I told him, honestly, that recently there had been times when I considered that after the trip to Italy, I might leave him. That was how frustrated I felt during those two weeks.

Just after the wedding, we caught an afternoon bus to Cancun - the day before our flight to Italy. After checking into our hotel, we headed out to our favorite local restaurant just around the corner. Returning to the hotel, we tried to get some sleep prior to the long flight from Cancun to Miami and on to Frankfurt, before heading into Milan. The trip was about to begin.

***

I had reservations about our trip. John seemed to want to fill every hour with visits to museums and historic sights, For my part, I concentrated on the recommended sights in Milan, like *The Last Supper* and *David*, the *Uffizi Gallery*, and the *Duomo* in Florence. In Venice, I booked nothing, leaving us to explore the city at leisure. I am not much for details. On the other hand, John had Rome's schedule well fleshed out. I like history and wanted to see all of the tourist sights as did he. I worried about his propensity for reading every page and sign in the museums. I tend to skim over things, whereas he digests every word in whatever language he is reading. Prior to the trip he began to study Italian to better prepare him to read "direction signs", so he said. He had purchased a Spanish-Italian language text!

On the flight from Miami we sat apart – the airlines choice, not ours. He enjoyed chatting with his seatmate while I sat writing about the past two weeks of our journey. My seatmate spoke only Italian. On a 747 it is easy to be alone when those around you do not speak your language. Even there I felt isolated, much like I had the previous two weeks in Progreso. I wondered about the month ahead. Except for the guys we had met on *Gaydar*, I wondered about my ability to communicate if no one spoke English. I had been told that the younger people all spoke English and Italian. At this point, I knew that Bob in Milan, Stefano in Florence and Mario in Rome spoke both languages! If and when we met up with them I would be okay.

We landed in Frankfurt, Germany, cleared customs and headed for our connecting flight to Milan. Arriving at Malpensa Airport, we took a shuttle into the city, getting off at the train station – except we had taken the wrong shuttle and ended up at the wrong station! With luggage in tow, we set out on foot, not yet confident enough to try the Metro or a taxi. It looked like Toronto, yet everyone spoke a foreign language – Italian. So much for asking young people for directions! Instead we bought a map – one problem – we had the name of our hotel but no address or phone number. All that we did know was that it was near Repubblica Metro stop...wherever that was.

After two hours of walking and dragging our luggage we found our hotel and trudged up the long flight of stairs. After checking in and surrendering our passports, we were shown our modest room. It had been a long flight from Cancun. We had left at 630 pm Milan time on November 6th. It was now after 1200 noon November 7th in Milan – 18 hours more or less. We were determined not to fall asleep, so we showered and headed out for our first Italian meal, do a little exploring and then come back and relax in bed. When we finished our little tour, it was after 8:00 pm.

We slept until 8:00 a.m. the next morning, had continental breakfast in the hotel, and headed for the train station – the one that was only six blocks away! We purchased our tickets on the Eurostar for Verona and Venice and when the time came, boarded the train.

The half day in Verona, followed by the six days in Venice were idyllic. I took pictures of everything I saw, much like a child in a toy store. We were both sponges trying to absorb all of the sights – *Saint Mark's Square* and *Basilica*, the *Doge's Palace*, a multitude of museums and, of course, the *Grand Canal.* At one hundred euros an hour, we dismissed the idea of a moonlight gondola ride. It wasn't a good idea for two guys to be seen snuggling in a gondola in Venice. The gay culture was non-existent, despite all of the statues of naked men everywhere, fully exposed to the elements. We were supposed to meet a gay Australian guy whom we had met online, but after playing telephone/email tag, we gave up on that happening.

We took the *vaporetti* (launch) to both Murano and Burano on subsequent days. Another day we toured a Picasso exhibit and the *Peggy Guggenheim Gallery.* We purchased two oil paintings of Venice and the Grand Canal. Deliberately, we avoided having a glass of wine in St. Mark's Square while listening to strings playing waltzes...way overpriced! One night we ate dinner beside the Canal with stars shining overhead while the gondoliers sang their hearts out for the tourists. It seemed like we were on a movie set.

On our last morning in Venice, we purchased our train tickets and left for Florence. There we had rented a house from Stefano for the five nights. I jokingly referred to him as our Italian houseboy

When we finally met Stefano later that evening, he turned out to be in his late thirties, thin, and actually quite handsome – certainly not a macho Italian stallion! So much for dreams.

The subsequent days were filled with walking, museums, galleries, shops, churches and more churches! After a while one tires of Madonnas with Child, although those naked statues of men always picked us up, unless a previous Pope or Cardinal had the penises broken off or covered with leaves! At least, David had been left intact. John did wonder about David. Wasn't he supposed to be Jewish?

John and I have never been to a gay bar of any kind, not that we saw any in Florence. We had a list from the Internet about which we had asked Stefano. Most were closed, or as best we could understand, seedy, in the American sense of the word. Oh well. On our second last night in Florence we went to see the Bed and Breakfast where we would be staying in when we returned after our week in Tuscany. The owners had sought us out on *Gaydar* and we had booked their place for one night. They both were in their late thirties, one French, the other from

Ecuador...neither was especially guapo. Hey, we only wanted a room at the B and B, nothing more.

Leaving Florence by car the next morning, we traveled through Tuscany towards Siena. Everywhere were olive groves, vineyards and cypress trees, and endless rolling hills. In summertime these would have been fields of sunflowers and poppies. Not so in mid-November, although it was unseasonably warm and sunny.

We were staying southwest of Siena at a small *agritourismo* – an Italian word for an apartment on a working farm. We had found this one while reading a popular tourist guide on Italy. When we finally reached there, it was everything it was supposed to be. The owner, a thirty-ish single Italian with very interesting features, was leaving...for Mexico the next morning! Another, oh well. As it was Sunday, all of the stores, gas stations and restaurants were closed – except one. Fate drew us there that night...

When we walked in we were impressed with the décor. There were lots of windows, gold drapes, an extensive wine display and a crackling fire in the fireplace. An Italian guy in his late thirties came walking out of the kitchen wearing a tight black T-shirt and tight black jeans. Good combination! On his T-shirt, the word, "BACI" – kiss in Italian, spelled out in rhinestones....mmm...very interesting. He seated us and mumbled something about talking to us later. Curious? He introduced himself as Paolo. Not another soul was in the restaurant..

He arrived back at our table with a bottle of Italian wine and three glasses. We attempted to chat using English, Spanish and Italian. Spanish seemed to work best. Our Italian was very meager. We seemed to make ourselves understood. He understood more English than he spoke – much like me and Spanish. He poured a small amount of wine in one glass and then swished it around and smelled it, checking its 'legs'. He then poured that into the second glass, repeating the process. Finally, he poured it into his glass and tasted it. He pronounced the wine undrinkable! He sent for a second bottle and repeated the process, this time satisfying himself that it was satisfactory. Thankfully, no more swishing.

By this time he knew our names as well. Sipping the wine along with us, we began to banter on. It turned out that he was actually the owner, so he did what he pleased. In a short time, our banter turned sexual, talking about Italian versus Mexican. By then we knew that he was gay for sure and that he, like us, had been married, but not now.

The meal and the conversation were wonderful. Upon leaving, we exchanged hugs and Italian kisses (cheeks). We asked if we could buy a loaf of bread for breakfast back at the agritourismo. Of course! Brazenly, I asked if he would deliver it to our place after he closed. What did I have to lose? He brought out the bread and said he hoped to see us again...

The next two days were spent exploring the Tuscan countryside, the hill towns of Volterra, San Gimignano, Chianti and Siena. On the evening of the second night, we went back to the restaurant for dinner with Paolo again.

He was very pleased to see us again – more hugs and Italian kisses. We sat down, again, in a basically empty restaurant, and the wine production started again. I followed his every move. Not being in a hurry to eat, we invited him to join us. He poured three glasses of wine and went to replace the cork. It fell on the floor by John's foot. Paolo reached down to get it, grabbing John's leg…for support. Right! We bantered on again and decided that we would let him surprise us with the food tonight.

What followed was an incredible five course meal, composed of antipasto – prosciutto, bufalo mozzarella, artichokes, four types of crostini, bruschetta, olives, bread, parmesan cheese, and salami and Pecorino cheese – native to Tuscany. Then came the *primi patti* - fresh artichoke lasagna and meat crepes. These were followed by the *secundi patti* – a meat board – sausage, roasted chicken, veal scaloppini, wild boar and slices of roast beef. This was followed by a small salad – Italian style. John, who always eats salads, passed. He was stuffed. The second bottle of wine did not help the feeling. We relaxed awhile, bantering and sipping the wine and then Paolo went into the kitchen and brought out espresso and Sambuca, but not before we had refreshed our palates with some very cold, local *limoncello* (lemon liqueur).

As it was getting late, we asked for our bill. Paolo returned with a piece of paper on which he had scribbled – 50 euros! What we had consumed was worth twice that price. We insisted he take more money. He insisted that if he did we would have to take another bottle of his favorite wine with us. Graciously, we accepted.

Thinking this would be the last time we would see him, we took the requisite photo, exchanged strong hugs and more forceful kisses and left the restaurant. Towards the end of our stay, more customers had arrived.

The combination of alcohol and three espressos kept me awake most of the night. In my head, I continued to play a new poem – dedicated to Paolo, entitled, "New Friends" - Dedicated to our new Italian friend – Paolo, November 22, 2006 -Costafabbri, Italy

Two too many espressos,
After a long, adventurous day!
Now I lie awake,
As lightning flashes,
Emblazoning the night.

My mind replays the scenic landscapes
Of the beautiful Tuscan hills,
Olive groves and vineyards –
Old medieval towns.

In life, no matter how prepared,
We cannot contemplate,
The many friends along the way,
Played by the hands of Fate.

Round each corner,
A friend awaits,
If you are ready to receive
A friendly smile, a warm embrace,
In an unexpected place.

The next two days we again traversed the Tuscan countryside – south to Montalcino, home to one of the world's best wines – Brunello, and another day to Chinciano Terme to tour an Etruscan museum. We were to head back to Florence with our rental car on the Friday. We had one last dinner with Paolo.

As it was, the last night at his place was very busy with locals. He went through the big wine production, took our orders, exchanged some friendly banter, but that was all he had time for that night. With our usual hugs and Italian kisses, we paid our bill. Before we left the restaurant, he insisted that we take along a bottle of his extra virgin olive oil. The label said "Paolo is thinking of you"…okay it was originally in Italian. I translated it.

After a good night's sleep we set out for our return to Florence the following morning, following a circuitous route east to Arezzo and northwest through the Chianti Region again, arriving in Florence in late afternoon. We parked the car near the B and B and then walked around Florence one last time. The next morning, we returned the rental car and were on the Eurostar headed to Rome.

***

We arrived in Rome and walked the six blocks to our hotel near Piazza Repubblica. It was a small place on the second floor, but al least it had an elevator. There were only eight rooms, under renovation. Since our room had just been painted, we could not check in just then – our room furniture was literally sitting in the street! We walked around for one and a half hours while they put our room back together. Of all of our accommodations, this was the smallest room, but we still had a private bath. Since the air was off we had to contend with the paint odors.

Our first night in Rome! We headed out on a self-guided walking tour. I was sure that John planned on seeing every tourist attraction before we went to bed! We walked down one of the main retail streets towards the *Roman Forum*. Our first historic site – *Trajan's Monument* – was not too impressive in the dark. Onwards towards the monument to Italy's first president, Vittorio Emanuele with its' chariots precariously perched on the top. From there, we walked to the piazza in front of the *Capitoline Museum*. Walking down the stairs, we bought a bag of roasted chestnuts and then on to the *Spanish Steps*. Inadvertently, we ended up at the *Trevi Fountain*. Gelato time… Not content, John had to find the Spanish Steps still.

All I wanted was to get back to our hotel. More walking. I convinced John to stop at an Internet café so that we could rest and check emails. In Mexico, we had arranged to meet a local guy our age for drinks or whatever. Responding to his email, I suggested that we meet the next evening…at the Spanish Steps, now that we knew where they were.

During the Rome portion of our trip, we had prebooked several tours – the *Colosseum* and *Forum*, a twilight tour of Rome, and a five hour tour of the *Vatican* and *St. Peter's Basilica* – all with the same company. On our first day, we had two tours planned, one in the morning and one at night. We met our first tour guide just outside the Colosseum the next morning. James was an American, from Florida, late 30's, handsome, charming, and as we soon learned – gay. He was a history major who had moved to Rome to be near his Italian wife and two children. They were not yet divorced, but he wanted to be near his kids, so he had moved here from Florida a few years earlier.

The Colosseum tour was amazing – just six of us, including James. Halfway through the morning tour, he let us know that the other three people were scheduled for another tour with him after lunch, a tour of the *Palatine Hills*, if we were interested. We jumped at the chance. James was an excellent guide. His knowledge of Roman history was incredible. Best of all, he had a fun manner of explaining the various sites.

At lunch, James, John and I sat together and shared life stories. At one point, James remarked, "Why am I telling you guys this?" The truth was, the night before he had broken up with his somewhat older partner of six months. James was hurting and we were there to listen. At that point, our Spirits had decided that we should be together, albeit briefly.

At the end of the tour, we said goodbye with the gay-customary hug and kiss. We invited James to join us for dinner or drinks after the twilight tour. He wasn't sure that he was up to socializing.

The twilight tour covered much of the same ground as John's first night tour, but with some otherwise unknown backstreet highlights. It was a long three hours. Approaching the Capitoline Museum once again, there was James!

We walked the streets back towards the Colosseum. James had pointed out his apartment building in the morning as we were standing inside the Colosseum. For a few minutes I thought that we might just go there for drinks and conversation. John was hungry, so we headed to one of James' favorite pizza places – gay-owned and gay clientele. At this hour of the evening there were only five patrons in total.

Over pizza and wine we discussed the challenges of being gay, the difficulties of ending a marriage when children were involved, and our individual journeys out of the closet. Too soon, it was time to leave. The restaurant was closing. After big, meaningful hugs, we parted company, with John and me heading back to our hotel to catch some sleep before our five hour Vatican tour the next morning. James was working another tour the next morning, unfortunately for us. He was a special guy. We would keep in touch. Someday we might just see James in Mexico!

Our tour guide of the Vatican, although knowledgeable, did not have James' charisma. It was a long day. We kept comparing him to James. After that, we headed back to our hotel, trying to find some of the places that we had seen the previous night, so we could take daytime photos. We surprised ourselves, finding many of them.

That night we decided on a late dinner and walked the back streets of Rome in search of a 'Mom and Pop' restaurant. We stumbled upon one. It was a small place. It was there that we met Sofia – a forty-ish woman who would introduce us to her favorite Italian restaurant the following night. We took an oath of secrecy not to tell any other tourists! There was no menu! Here is what the meal included –

8 antipasto dishes
2 bottles of red wine
Pasta with lobster AND shrimp
Caesar salad
A variety of fruits and cheeses
Gelato between courses to cleanse the palate
Espresso
Unlimited liqueurs, including limoncello, Proseco and amaretto with the bottles being placed on our table…

The total bill was 75 Euros!!! No wonder we were sworn to secrecy…

Before we left Rome, we toured the old Roman port of *Ostia Antica* and the *Borghese Gallery*.

The former would turn out to be better than Pompeii and the latter was outstanding with its wonderful collection of art treasures, many of which had been coerced out of the hands of the artists by blackmail and coercion from the church hierarchy.

We left Rome, vowing to return for a longer period of time. The four days were not enough, but we needed to head for Sorrento and the final week of our trip. We boarded another Eurostar for the ride south to Naples. One hour out of Rome I remembered that we had locked our Canadian passports in the hotel's safe. We couldn't go back. We needed those three days later for our flight back to Milan. From Naples, we took another train, the *Circumvesuviana*, to Sorrento.

***

We arrived finding the weather very pleasant and warm for late November. The city was beautifully decorated for Christmas. White lights were strung across the streets. A huge Christmas tree stood proudly in *Piazza Tasso*. There were palm trees festooned with the same lights. We were awed by the city on first impression.

The B and B which we had booked was centrally located not far from the water. We explained our problem with the passports and the proprietor graciously offered to call Rome and have them expressed to us the next day! Shortly after we arrived, three other guests arrived – Americans. It turned out that they were an aunt and he nephew, and her nephew's friend. We introduced ourselves and that evening, the four guys *sans aunt* went out for a walk and a quiet dinner. The next morning, the four of us were off to climb *Mount Vesuvius* and to explore the ruins of *Pompeii*.

We had a great time together, albeit the climb of Vesuvius was challenging! The vista of Naples below was incredible. That evening we decided to catch up on our laundry. We took turns riding shotgun at the local Laundromat. When it came my turn, one of the other guys decided to stay and talk. He confided in me that he was bisexual, although his friend, the nephew was straight. We talked about being gay for almost an hour while the clothes spun dry. Nothing occurred – just talk. I felt like, just maybe, I was mentoring him. When the laundry was done we both returned to the B and B, never mentioning our conversation.

We had been traveling in Italy for nearly three weeks. We had met two really nice gay guys – one in Rome, James, and the other near Siena, Paolo. Our anticipated encounters with other guys never occurred.

On our last day in Sorrento we took the ferry to *Capri*, to explore the famous Blue Grotto, Anacapri and Capri. Have I already used the word, 'idyllic'? It was totally awesome as we stood on the shores of the Gulf of Salerno, looking down on *Isola Faraglioni*.

With us were two new friends, Chas and Emily, whom we had met getting off the Circumvesuviana in Sorrento. They were a young American couple now living in Amsterdam, but were enjoying a short holiday in Sorrento. The four of us had signed on to this tour of Capri. Who goes to Capri without visiting the famous *"Blue Grotto"*? This being December entry would normally be dubious with rough seas. Together with Chas and Emily we boarded a small boat ducking down to enter the Grotto. It was breathtakingly beautiful! We all had lunch together and got to know each other that afternoon. As we stood there, both Chas and John were misty eyed. I wondered what each was thinking, as I snapped photos of the two men looking out over the Bay.

We separated for the rest of the tour. Eventually, John and I headed back to Sorrento on the ferry.

Surprisingly, that night, John and I were having dinner at a nearby restaurant when Chas and Emily walked in. I jokingly asked if they were there for a romantic meal or did they want to sit with a couple of old gay guys? Both, without hesitation, opted to have dinner with us. At the end of the night we exchanged email addresses and have since kept in touch.

The next morning we were off to Naples by bus to catch a flight back to Milan, where we would spend our last three days.

***

Upon arrival in Milan we went directly to the same hotel from where we had started. We had previously been chatting with a gay American, about fifty-five years old, who was now living in

Milan. We gave him a call and planned to meet for lunch the following day. We arranged to meet him at the nearby train station. This one we knew how to find.

The next morning, we had a light breakfast at the hotel and walked around Via Buenos Aires in the rain. At 12:30 we went to the train station to finally meet Bob, who was a little late. He was taller than we expected. Our first impression was good, but, of course, guarded.

We walked to lunch at a small Sicilian restaurant behind the station which had been recently opened. It was in a small gay conclave (Milan apparently has no gay neighborhood, even though 1000+ guys were listed on *Gaydar*). There were three gay-owned businesses on the street, the restaurant, a video store, and gay magazine office. Bob apparently had eaten many meals here. We were all greeted by Davide, the owner, with the traditional hugs and kisses on the cheek. At this time, there were not many patrons in the restaurant.

We ordered a bottle of wine, continuing to chat with Bob about his work, Milan, and his life as an HIV positive guy. He had only been in Milan eight months, but it was clear that he had many experiences with Italian men! Scanning the menu, we chose a wonderful pasta 'maccherona alla Norma' and were not disappointed. Aside from Paolo's in Siena, this was the best food that we had in Italy! Graciously, Bob picked up the check.

After lunch he took us on the Milan Metro and we headed downtown for a little personalized tour, taking in the *Duomo, Via Dante*, etc. As it was still raining, we hopped back on the Metro and headed for Bob's apartment. I wasn't sure what would happen. As it was, we simply chatted, until it was time to get some dinner.

It was now close to eight o'clock in the evening. Off we went to another of Bob's favorite restaurants for sandwiches and beer. From there we caught the Metro and left Bob, getting off at our stop near the Repubblica Metro Station. It had been a long and rainy day.

The next morning we walked around Milan doing some sightseeing and a little shopping. We had seen silk boxers in Rome and Florence which featured the midsection of Michelangelo's 'David'. There were the original sized ones and the ones with an 'enhanced' David. We though it would be fun to give our friend Willie (in Mexico) a pair. After much looking around, we did find the last pair anywhere. We had a planned city tour the next day, which included seeing da Vinci's *The Last Supper*. This day was another self-guided one. After four hours, we headed back to our hotel, before meeting Bob once again at the Sicilian restaurant – Davide's place.

We arrived before he did, so we sat and chatted at the bar with Davide. He wasn't our type either, but he was a nice young guy. We suspected that he and Bob may have had occasion to meet outside the restaurant, but nothing was ever said. This night there were more people in the restaurant – all obviously gay. Bob arrived about one half hour later. We left the bar and took a table in the front window of the restaurant so we could watch the men walk by.

Before we had ordered the wine, a twenty-something guy came in alone. He wasn't Italian and certainly was not bad looking. Not surprisingly, Bob knew him and introduced us to him. His name was Raoul and he was from Romania. He sat down at our table and ordered a drink. In his broken English, he told us that he had a fifteen year old wife back in Romania, and a child. In fact, as he stated, he was bisexual. The picture became clearer. He was obviously hustling the three of us. We continued to chat and eventually we ordered dinner, inviting him to join us.

When we left the restaurant, we said our goodbyes out front. Bob stood talking with Raoul as we walked away. I thought I knew where this would lead – right straight back to Bob's apartment! We headed back to our hotel for the night.

On our last day in Milan, we walked around and went on our planned tour which included the visit to Leonardo da Vinci's *The Last Supper*. We had managed to get the last tickets before we left Mexico. It had turned cold and began to drizzle again. When the tour stopped at the Duomo, we were surprised to see Bob walk by. Stopping to say a few last words, I asked about Raoul. I was wrong! Bob had gone home alone after talking to Raoul in front of the restaurant.

The next morning, we caught the shuttle to the airport at six o'clock in the morning, and flew to Frankfurt. With security high, every passenger was subjected to a full body 'frisk' by either a male or female agent. They were serious! From there we were off to Boston, Miami and then Cancun. We arrived back in Cancun twenty-four hours after leaving Milan! The tour was coming to an end.

***

We arrived back in Mexico at the beginning of December, spending two days in Playa Del Carmen before returning home to Progreso. As in the previous year, my daughters and their husbands and children had come in on a cruise ship for one day. We spent a relaxing day at the beach in Cozumel with them. It was great to see the grandkids again after two months absence. We had last seen them in Canada at the beginning of October.

Back home in Progreso we began the preparations for Christmas, anticipating the arrival on Christmas Eve of John's thirty-two year old son from Canada. This would be their first Christmas together in almost fifteen years. I knew that John was anxious. Of course, there was a lot to do. Every year we send out over one hundred Christmas cards – electronically. It takes time to correct addresses and enter new ones to the mailing list. Then there was the outside decorating to be done, shopping for presents and groceries.

There were less than two weeks to go before the arrival of Jeremy, John's son. Our focus turned to getting ready for Christmas and his arrival.

Christmas Eve finally arrived – *Noche Buena* in Mexico. We were having a midnight supper with Francisco and Gloria and their family. At ten o'clock we picked up Jeremy at the airport and returned home to start the celebrations. This was our second *Noche Buena* and our second Christmas in Mexico, far from my Canadian family. John at least had Jeremy. I was happy for him. Nevertheless, the sights and sounds of

Christmas always have made me feel sad and lonely. Christmas would never be my favorite time of year!

***

While we had been away from Progreso, there had been some changes. Our gossipy, gringo grandma, Eleanor, had returned to Texas for good! We had an email expressing her pleasure at being back in civilization. She never let up. She wouldn't be missed in Progreso!

Dani's husband Chad had decided to go back to Korea, leaving her and the two teenage boys here in Progreso. Before he left, they moved to a new, less expensive apartment off the beach over a nursery school. They were downsizing. He never had learned much Spanish here, nor had he found any work that paid him. As for Dani, she continued to teach English four hours a week in Progreso, but she had also found work in the city, teaching at a university part-time.

Then there was Ross, our Texan friend. When we last saw him, he had leased a house down from us. He had a new business – property management and home renovations. While we were gone, there had been some renovations at his house. His long-time girlfriend had moved out just after he had a birthday party where a rather large female stripper was the entertainment. He'd gotten carried away and had indulged himself with more than a lap dance. It was likely the last straw for his girlfriend. At the moment he was all alone and playing the field again. Some guys never learn!

A few days before Christmas, George and Alyce had reappeared. We were at the local hotel for Happy Hour when they walked in. Everyone was rather shocked. The last we had heard was that they were in North Carolina, where George was supposedly engaged as a professor at a small university which his daughter was attending. Alyce was not working. They had left the hotel in the hands of a trusted Mexican employee. Before they had left, they had closed the restaurant and now only rented rooms and sometimes opened the bar at night. In this season, when the snowbirds began to return, the room business normally would pick up.

When they walked in, they began chatting with a few people, working the room. They had some friends still in Progreso whom they had not cheated or taken advantage of. For obvious reasons, they avoided John and I...Dani was seated beside us! For the next forty-five minutes they sat completely alone at the bar, like the royal couple in residence. No one gave them the time of day. With their backs to the room, they were the center of gossip. We learned from another longtime snowbird that George was involved in a beachfront condo project now, which most expected would never ever see groundbreaking. Even still, George had taken several deposits on the $200,000 units according to the rumors. He was still wheeling and dealing with other people's money. When Happy Hour ended, and the music stopped, most people left – neither George nor Alyce did, however.

As they say, the more things change, the more they stay the same.

***

To the uninitiated, Progreso has constant weather all year long – sun. After you have lived here a while, there are some obvious signals that the season is changing. The *nortes* – north winds – begin to blow in late December, usually. These strong winds from the Gulf of Mexico blow sand and garbage everywhere. At times, the blowing sand is actually biting. Every morning, work crews sweep the stretch along the *malecón*, returning the sand to the beach once again. They actually keep track of the nortes much like the north keeps track of tornadoes. This particular year they started early, and by the time New Year's came along they were numbering in the 30's. Thankfully we had been spared any hurricanes. The water temperature drops to near Great Lakes summer temperatures - 60's – no Mexican goes into the water unless there is lots of sun. The *nortes* are very drying – plants need constant watering. Floors need lots of sweeping with the blowing sand and grit. Windows are always dirty.

As the number of *nortes* diminishes, south winds make their presence known – often resulting in warmer daytime temperatures and rain. About this same time, the deciduous trees – almendres, crotons, etc. may lose their leaves. More debris amidst the street garbage… Raking is futile until all of the leaves have fallen, leaving bare branches. In our area, the produce in the markets changes – another sign of a new season.

New Year's Eve came and went quickly. John's son attended a small NYE party with us at one of Dani's friends. Cyndee was an American film producer who lived in Mexico most of the year. At the moment it was a convenient base for her to use for easy access to Cuba, where she was working on a documentary film about Cuban music and dance. At this writing, the average American was forbidden by the government from going to Cuba, no matter what country they went from. Cuban travel was illegal and Cyndee knew the risk.

Right after January 1st, the flocks of snowbirds began to return. One of the first pair to return was Bobbi and Dick from Western Canada. This year they had chosen to stay at a small residential hotel on the other side of town. After the previous year's experience, we were content with their decision, although we had made all of the arrangements for them since we were living here.

By now it had been about three months since we had been to Canada. I had last seen my family in Cozumel at the beginning of December. John had been talking to a Canadian friend and was thinking that it was time to fly back up for a visit. As it turned out, the 78 year old father of his friend had a skiing accident the previous January. He and his wife were visiting Toronto and John felt it was a good time to go north. They were from British Columbia. Another of their daughters who lived near them in BC was going on an extended holiday to Southeast Asia. When they returned to BC, the old couple would have no one to assist them in their daily routines. John and I discussed the situation and he contacted his friend's mother directly and offered to fly west for one week. Since it would be too costly for both of us, and John had Air Miles, we decided that he should go alone. In all he would take three weeks – one to be in BC and the other two to visit friends and family in Ontario. Finding a great airfare from Cancun to Detroit, I decided that I would surprise my youngest daughter and go north for her thirty-third birthday in mid-February. John and I would meet there and fly back to Mexico on the 19th of February. Since we had been in Progreso we had never been separated except for his overnight in the hospital when he had undergone the minor surgery. It would be very different for each of us.

I was naturally apprehensive. John would be gone eight days before I left. Using what we had learned from our trip to Italy, John proceeded to make contact with guys in British Columbia who could advise him of how to get where he needed to go from the airport in BC. The difference this time was that he was traveling alone. When he started to get responses suggesting more than sharing info about his transportation queries, I was concerned. That little jealous voice started to whisper in my ear. John never hid the messages as far as I knew. He was very open about them. Why was I worried?

Just after the New Year I had accepted a four month job in the city, for which I had previously applied, but had been rejected. The person who got the job had developed a very dangerous case of Hepatitis B and would be unable to return to work for at least four months. Hesitantly I had accepted the appointment. I had told John that I needed a purpose in Progreso besides writing. A door had opened...Spirit had intervened and granted my wish. Now the tables were turned. John was at home all day while I was working. Unlike the previous situation when he worked for only two hours a day, I would be away from the casa almost eight hours, four days a week! How would he occupy his time in my absence? He assured me that he had lots of work around the house. Of course, I was projecting on him what I had sometimes done in his absence.

It was shortly after starting work that I first met Donna from northern California. She had arrived to explore the city as a potential future home for her and her husband, Carl. In the course of her 50+ years, she had worked doing various things. She was a professional artist, chef, restaurateur and author of a cookbook! She had attended university in Berkeley. Need I say more? She was such a neat lady...

A few months later I met her friends from the same area, also in pursuit of their future home. Connie and Sheila would eventually purchase a home just a few doors from my work.

Donna and Carl did buy also – about fifteen blocks away from Connie and Sheila. We all became quite good friends as they began the remodeling of their respective new homes. John and I had keys to each of their houses and had a bedroom in each where we could crash whenever we wanted to stay overnight in the city.

When John had been teaching here and I stayed home, I had chatted with guys during the day. For all I knew, he could be doing the same. Chatting was less dangerous than real sex! Hadn't I told my wife that before I met John?

I chatted with guys in Mexico, but never met any of them. Why shouldn't he do the same if he wanted to? Would I ever get past the feelings of fear that he might actually hook up with someone else while I was out of the house each day? The same went for his upcoming trip to BC. I felt that John was absolutely faithful to me, and yet, what if?

I guess that part of my concern was in knowing that there were gay couples who actually played separately. I assumed that their rule was "Don't ask and don't tell." That bothered me, and yet if it worked for them, both of them, I could not condemn it. As far as I knew, John had never played alone since we arrived in Mexico. Although I had been tempted, the same went for me. It was always exciting to think about it, but when it came right down to meeting someone, I chose not to do so, out of love and respect for John.

The other factor was being together 24/7. Honestly, there weren't many opportunities. With John away in Canada, and me alone in Mexico, we might be challenged in our faithfulness to each other.

***

John left twelve days before me, heading to Cancun to catch his flight north to Detroit. From there, he would cross the international border and head for Toronto where he would catch a flight west to British Columbia. It wasn't an easy goodbye for me. I agonized about his leaving, and being alone in Progreso. I worried about guys he might meet when he got to BC. It didn't help that he had been making contact with a couple of guys on '*gay.com*' and that he had changed his passwords on both AOL and Hotmail without telling me. We had always known each other's passwords from day one! In Cancun, he stayed in a different hotel from the one we normally used. Why? Add up those three and you can understand my trepidation about him going alone.

John had explanations for each one.

A – He needed to find out how to get from the airport in BC to the place where he was staying the week.

B – He received a notification from AOL advising him to change his passwords for security reasons.

C – The new hotel was closer to the bus station in Cancun.

All were very logical.

While he was away he phoned or emailed regularly. He told me about a guy he met in BC and about a house party they went to…separate cars. I had encouraged him to go after all! I had seen a picture of the guy on 'gay.com'. He had told me to check a profile of another guy he had talked with online and who was also at the party. Torture! When he got home from the party, he phoned me in Mexico to tell me all that had occurred. According to him, just a group of older guys who spent the night talking and drinking, not even any good movies.

As always I wondered, would I ever get past these unfounded worries? I hated those feelings of insecurity, but didn't seem to be able to get past them. One afternoon, I decided to head for the beach to soak up some sun. I decided to take pen and paper with me just in case I got an inspiration. As I looked across the water, I saw the lighthouse at the end of the pier. I thought about John. For the last three years, he had been my lighthouse! He helped me to stay focused and continuously guided me on this journey when I felt I was running aground in my life. In my soul's dark moments he was there for me! My light never seemed as bright when he was not around. Pen in hand, I wrote the following poem –

Lighthouse

For centuries,
Lighthouses have stood –
Beacons in the night,
And in the daylight,
For ships and sailors alike.

Majestically,
They weather storms and squalls,
And guide ships through those storms,
Never expecting anything in return.
Silent in the darkness,
Except for an occasional foghorn,
Sending out a warning,
When danger is imminent.

Some of us
Have a personal lighthouse,
Which like those which dot the coastlines,
Are beacons in our lives,
Warn us of imminent dangers,
When we might otherwise,
Ignore the consequences,
Of going off course,
Straying.
Distracted by our actions,
In the dark moments of our lives.

MY lighthouse stands proudly
Beside me.
He turns on his light for me,
Continuing to guide me
Through the channels
Of my life.

Together,
My lighthouse and I
Can weather any storms,
And will continue to do so,
Sailing on through the darkness,
Until daylight re-appears,
On the eastern horizon.

As for me I busied myself with my new job – spending more than the required time trying to keep my self busy and off the computer. When I did come home I would check emails and go on the chat lines.

One night I chatted with a 29 year old guy from the city, Alberto, whom we had met through a mutual friend. We knew him socially, but liked his company. He was in the second year of architectural school and was doing very well in his studies. He was working on a project for an upcoming exhibition in Mexico City. After talking for a while, he emailed me the sketches thus far. They were very good.I asked about the cost of participating, etc. While chatting I got an inspiration. He was short of funds to pay for the travel and accommodation for the one week trip. What if I could get some other gay friends to put some money in a 'pot' to help finance the trip? He was overwhelmed by the idea that 'extrañeros' might do something like this for a young Mexican gay guy without any strings attached, or wanting sexual favors in return! I assured him that I would TRY to raise some funds. That night I sent off a dozen emails to other gay men whom we had acquaintances with in the city, explaining my idea. I was happy when I got a couple of responses from guys who were willing to donate money based on my just asking, without specific details. As for the other gay guys I was disappointed. Were they as shallow as their stereotypes? One thought I should start a foundation. Give me a break! I wanted to do something anonymously and without bureaucracy. By the time I set up a foundation it would be too late for Alberto. I persevered and came up with eighty percent of his needs. (Just before he left for the exhibition, with John and I back in Mexico, I gave him the money I had collected…no strings attached!)

I continued working for the days leading up to my departure for Cancun. Each day there was usually an email from John and/or a phone call depending on my work hours. We were two time zones apart. I was relieved when he flew from BC back to Toronto, even though initially, he was staying with a former girlfriend. We had met on several occasions. You can guess what was going on in my mind. One day he visited the Gay Village in downtown Toronto. He was shopping for some 'necessities' to bring back to Mexico.

Mercifully the day came for me to take the bus to Cancun. John had booked me a room in the hotel where he had stayed near the bus station.

When I arrived I found my way from the station to the hotel. I was staying in exactly the same room as John had used two weeks earlier. Again, you can imagine what went through my mind. After getting settled in, I set out for an Internet café. After checking my email I headed off to our favorite restaurant, dining alone. I sat watching the men go by. Four margaritas, two coffees and a Sambuca later, I headed back to the Internet café. I trudged back to the hotel to sleep – visions of previous occurrences in the room flashed through my overactive mind. In the morning, I got dressed and caught a bus to the airport. I was finally on my way to Detroit and Canada. Only five more days and nights without John! Once in the air, my thoughts once again turned to John.

How would he spend these last five nights? Another poem sprang forth. Of course the perennial theme…was worrying about John and what he might be doing alone in Toronto.

Worry

I wish I did not worry so
Those times when we are apart,
For I am certain that you love me
From the bottom of your heart!

And yet, when I am all alone
Those images appear
Of you, alone, with someone else, and
I am paralyzed with fear!

I do not like the feeling,
I can't wish it away,
I say, "Let go, let God"
Each and every day!

What must you say?
What must you do?
I wish I knew the answer
I'm affirming that "Let go, let God"
Will cure this insidious
Cancer.

Strange, I never ever use rhyme in my poetry. It seemed more like a Hallmark card when I had finished!

***

I arrived in Detroit and was met by Ralph, our old friend, and you will remember, one of John's former buddies, before we met. John knew that I was spending the night with Ralph. I wondered what he was thinking about this arrangement. I knew what I would be thinking in his shoes. Ralph gave me a big bear hug as we headed off to his nearby apartment. He and I had never been alone even though we had known each other for almost three years now. Of course, in the beginning I had harbored thoughts about the two of us...until John came into my life. Ralph was still struggling with his sexual identity.

Recently he had met a 'friend', Don, with whom he was spending considerable time. He was starting to talk more like a gay man. They spent many weekends at Don's place in Western Michigan. He stressed that, at this point, the relationship was purely platonic. Right! What was the old saying I had heard? "You can't get to second base with one foot still on first...."

Ralph had decided that we should eat in and had made a terrific pot roast. I splurged and found a great red wine from Australia. After dinner we watched both hockey and basketball. This was Detroit after all. Ralph kept flipping from one to another. I was beginning to think he was nervous. Shortly after midnight we called it an evening, with me sleeping in Ralph's bed. Okay, okay...he slept on the couch in his living room all night. Who knows – maybe visions of sugarplums danced in both our heads? Certainly the idea of sharing a bed with Ralph was intriguing. John knew that from past experience. Friendship prevented that from occurring, by mutual, unspoken, understanding, no doubt. The next morning, after a little shopping, Ralph took me across the border to my oldest daughter's home, where I would wait for John's return on Valentine's Day. Appropriate eh?

Back in my hometown, I spent time with my grand kids before John returned. It was extremely cold in February, but little snow as of yet. Thankfully. On the first Sunday back home, I crossed the border again to attend Church and have lunch with our good friend, Christina, who had visited us in Progreso the previous year. On my way back to Canada, I stopped and bought a birthday cake for my youngest daughter. She was turning thirty-three! I had come home to Canada to celebrate her birthday. Her mother, my "still-wife" was in Florida on vacation with her older sister.

On the Tuesday it began to snow. John had decided to come in a day early. I booked a hotel and rented a car for the duration of our stay. His train was delayed one half hour. What was one half hour after waiting almost two weeks?

When he arrived, it was just like that time almost three years ago when I had met him on the way to Mexico for the first time. We went straight to the hotel. It was so wonderful to be together again! He brought me two sweetheart teddy bears in honor of Valentine's Day. All I really needed was him. We spent the next two days at the hotel and then made an appointment with our massage therapist friend for a massage the following Friday.

The next Sunday we were back to Church in Detroit. We had spent two nights at my wife's house while she was away. On the Saturday we cooked a family dinner for my daughters and their families. On Sunday, my two daughters drove us back to Ralph's apartment to spend the last night before flying back to Mexico on Monday afternoon.

Once back in Cancun, we shared the room at the 'new' hotel, had dinner together at our favorite restaurant, and went to bed early. The next morning we caught the early bus from Cancun back home to Progreso. Home. This was six days before John's sixty-third birthday.

***

Back in Progreso, many snowbirds had returned. Bobbi and Dick were back. Eleanor wasn't returning. She was in Georgia. Chad left Dani and the boys and had gone back to Canada with the hopes of going back to the Far East, to earn some much needed cash. George and Alyce were still in North Carolina. There was no sign of Ross. Willie's mother and stepmother were visiting from England for the month. Nothing much had changed with our landlord's family.

I went back to my part time job, only to learn that the previous administrator had resigned and gone back to California. I was asked to take over the position long term. As John was back teaching in Progreso, I made a proposal to the Board which they ultimately accepted. I agreed to stay on until the end of the year to give them some continuity, with a six week vacation in the summer, so we could travel to Canada. Did I mention that I accepted a raise in salary?

Mid-March saw the arrival of one of John's lady friends and her sister-in-law from near Toronto. They were visiting the real Mexico for the first time. For eleven days, we would be hosts and tour guides. While I continued to work, John would be their guide. On the third day of their visit, John and I hosted our second annual snowbird BBQ. In attendance were Francisco, Gloria, Tomas and twenty or so other snowbirds, including our guests. There were seven Canadian couples, all straight as far as we knew. John BBQ'd. The other guests brought salads. Our houseguests made sangria. This would be the last big event of the winter season. After that, most would migrate north for another year.

We had a great afternoon, eating and drinking. At one point, our gay doctor friend from New Jersey leaned over and asked me how many guests knew that John and I were gay? Was he serious? They all did! From day one, John and I had always been open to everyone. What was there to hide anymore? I jokingly introduced our two female house guests as John and my wives from Canada. One guest incredulously believed it!

The next evening the four of us went into the city to see the Cuban Ballet production of Copelia. We had dinner first at our favorite restaurant. As the production lasted until 11:30 pm, we planned on staying at our friend, Willie's hotel in Centro. The ladies did have their own room this time.

In the morning, we toured the city on a double-decker bus (our first time since arriving here).

The next day, John took our guests to tour the ruins at *Uxmal* and *Kabah*. They planned on having lunch at our friend, Anna's, recently opened restaurant along the route. I stayed at home, as I had work to do as part of my job. Of course, I took a few breaks and chatted online with some buddies, including Ralph in Michigan.

***

John had increased his teaching hours while I continued working three days at my administrative job. For my part, I felt satisfaction with work. I finally had a purpose here. Personally, I regretted our time apart as he worked the same three days as I did, but he also worked four nights a week for three hours, which left me alone. I did have work to do at home, but it didn't keep me completely occupied during his absence. My poetry writing was once again halted. I wasn't spending much time on my book. I had never been a TV watcher. That was good, as we only received ten channels; nine were in Spanish! Needless to say, I usually ended up on the Internet!

On occasion I would talk with Alberto, the Mexican architectural student in the nearby city whom we had befriended. John and I had met him through a friend. The four of us had attended the symphony one night. We befriended him as he had no father. He was struggling with his sexual identity – it is very difficult being a young, gay professional here. While John was away in Canada, Alberto and I had coffee once to make arrangements for his trip to Mexico City.

On Sundays, Dani started to join us for the Internet church service from Michigan. She was struggling with being a single parent since Chad had returned to Canada. The church services seemed to bring her some peace. After nineteen years of marriage, there was the stress of trying to maintain a long distance relationship again. Chad's father died after he went back to Canada and Chad was now living with his mother to help her out. When he tried to go back to the Far East, he was denied a work visa. His *balls* had dropped in Canada for the time being. Their future together did not look good. Dani had no intention of leaving Mexico!

It was fast approaching *Semana Santa* in Mexico – Holy Week/Easter. As always, that would mean many more people at the beach, as well as music 'til all hours of the night! While John would not be working, I would, as we did not close down the office for the holidays, just Good Friday.

John invited Alberto to spend the weekend with us in Progreso. After much consideration, he agreed. It was a great three days, just relaxing, chatting and watching TV, including our Sunday church service. Alberto seemed to enjoy it all. For Easter dinner, the three of us went out for sushi. By this time, Alberto was referring to us as his two fathers – Dad and Pops. We were proud that he felt that way about us. Indeed, we had begun to think of him as a son. The three of us had a memorable weekend.

After Easter, John started back teaching again, or should I say was supposed to. Sometime during the night, he became very sick and spent most of the next three days in bed. Finally, he was ready to go back to work! As is always the case when he is ill, I worry about his health even more so. What if? I agonize about our future. As John didn't feel up to it, we spent several nights on opposite sides of the bed. I missed the closeness we usually shared. Even after he appeared to recover his strength, things were not the same between us. Hopefully, this would change as he regained his stamina after the illness. The proverbial time would tell.

I wrote several long letters to a gay friend in Florida, whom I had actually never met in person. We corresponded every other week or so. 'Terry' and his longtime partner had visited Progreso a year ago. A mutual acquaintance gave them my email address and phone number, but we never connected while they were here. Since then, we'd share trials and tribulations. Terry was HIV+, but it was under control. His partner, approximately the same age, was always traveling, looking for their retirement home outside the USA. Terry's parents, although in their eighties, were both very much of concern to him, in spite of his own physical problems. In a sense, we became alter egos. John knew of Terry and often read the emails. Terry was very spiritual as well and we often chatted about our personal journeys. I could never quite figure out him and his partner's relationship. The partner never seemed to work. Maybe he was involved in property management. Strange, I never asked. One moment they were looking at a property in Mexico, the next in Costa Rica, more recently Nicaragua. The bottom line for Terry, being HIV+, was accessibility to US medical treatment should the need arise after he retired in two years.

Terry was going through a stressful period at work. His partner continued trips in search of their retirement home, often taking a 'friend'. Terry was feeling anxious about the relationship too. At one point, a younger guy came on to him. Terry was confused and tempted. He sent me a long email, explaining his angst. As he often did with me, I was able to get him to focus. I couldn't help but think that, just as there is AA for alcoholics, there should be something similar for gay men in relationships. The idea for Homosexuals Anonymous – HA! – made me smile in amusement. Surely, in 2007, there were enough gay couples where one or the other partner had been tempted to seek out other men! Maybe Terry and I were the seeds of that new association?

One morning, John awoke early. He hadn't slept well. During an uncommon dream, he had been contemplating his future health. What if? What followed was a two hour discussion of what we were still doing in Progreso after almost three years, and what might happen if we moved back to Canada in the foreseeable future.

> Where would we live?
> How could we afford to live?

This was the first time that we had ever had this discussion. We had always affirmed, especially with my family back in Canada, that we would stay in Mexico as long as we were able to. Deep down, I wondered whether this was the reason behind John's lack of interest in daily life, his fatigue, his aloofness.

***

I knew that out of the darkness comes light. From time to time, like the Mexican poinsettia, it is necessary to go back into the darkness in order to produce a beautiful flower. So it seemed with John. While he had been in the dark, I had busied myself with work and reading four lengthy novels – two mysteries by popular authors, one fictional account of the Maya, and a fourth – *The Secret Supper* which revolved around the secret messages in Leonardo da Vinci's *The Last Supper* in Milan, which John and I had seen in our trip to Italy before Christmas. John had turned inward; I had chosen different vehicles to get me through this dark period. Interesting that it is usually me who internalizes things.

It had been almost a month since John's initial dream. While outwardly he appeared bored with no meaningful work to keep him occupied during my three times a week absence, I suspected some deeper emotional struggle.

We were planning our annual trip to Canada, but John was unsure when? How long? Could we afford it? None of those concerned me, especially the latter. Had we not accepted that our periodic visitations were a part of living in Mexico? Of course it was costly to fly or drive, but eleven months of the year we lived economically in Mexico! The trip to Italy had long been paid for. For me, the possibility of seeing my daughters and grand children enabled me to dismiss the cost of the trip. John had no such 'reward', once we got to Canada. Neither of his sons were that close to him, although we hoped to see his youngest son, albeit likely briefly. Essentially we were going to be house sitting a friend's place for two weeks. The rest of the time, we'd be visiting my family and other friends in Southern Ontario.

A few days later, Anna called to let us know that she was coming to Progreso for the weekend. John and Anna had taken the same course in Canada to teach English as a Second Language. She had arrived shortly after John in 2003. After teaching for a short time in a small town south of the city, she had decided to buy a piece of property near Uxmal to develop her own restaurant. She had sold everything in Canada and invested her life savings in the project. On first seeing the cement block structure I was stunned! Here she was approaching sixty years of age and she as starting her own business, seemingly in the middle of nowhere. To top it off, she lived alone! This lady had *balls*!

It was the slow season in the restaurant business. It was also election weekend in the Yucatan. This meant no alcohol sold in stores and restaurants for forty-eight hours! No liquor equals no business. We hadn't seen her since her sixtieth birthday in March. I personally looked forward to her visit. John would have someone other than me to talk to about his concerns. She was always a positive person and was herself, on a spiritual journey. She was quick to see that John was not his usual self. We talked about what had been occurring lately.

The night she arrived was our landlord's son, Tomas' twenty-sixth birthday fiesta. Bad timing! Fifty or sixty people had been invited. Francisco and Gloria spent the day preparing for the event. Tomas was excited. Gloria was happy to have something to do. She had been in Playa Del Carmen for several weeks helping her oldest daughter and her Italian husband get ready to open their restaurant there. And...when it was opened she was likely going to go back and help them more! Francisco would have to fend for himself without her. She had seized the opportunity to work in Playa where she knew she would be appreciated.

The party went on until five-thirty IN THE MORNING, with John, Anna and I grabbing sleep as best we could with the ongoing talking and music outside our windows. We all woke up tired. The day dragged on with a brief visit to the beach. After dinner, we watched a comedy movie (to lighten up John). He had been quiet all day. When Anna went to bed, he and I sat and had another of our long conversations. We were both stressed. I suggested that maybe he needed time alone. He declined. Perhaps, a spiritual retreat? Maybe. Nothing was resolved. I tried to get him to focus on the NOW, the Present, which I had been reading about in Eckhart Tolle's latest book, *A New Earth*. I wasn't sure that it made any difference. I voiced my concern about our no longer seeming to be on the same path. Amidst tears, his and mine, we professed our ongoing love for each other. I had been where John now was, on several occasions. I identified with his confusions, his concerns. We both knew that, like me, he had to work this through on his own. We each have to do our own work in life. Our individual happiness is up to ourselves!

The following day, Anna returned to her place. Nothing had really been changed by her visit.

***

Coincidentally, John began to feel better. He started to take early morning walks after I left for work. During the day, he busied himself with work for his English classes which he was teaching again. When I came home from work he seemed less distant. We had also booked the summer trip to Canada – no more putting it off. We agreed to shorten it to four weeks rather than six and a half, thereby cutting our expenses. I had investigated a car rental – seven hundred dollars Canadian for one month! I hadn't told him about that expense yet. I had hoped we could manage by using the car at the house we were 'sitting' and only having to rent for two weeks, or, with luck, being able to borrow one of my daughter's vehicles. We would wait and see.

While I had thought things were improving just a little, the week after Anna's visit, John and I had several more discussions. I tried so hard to remain positive and supportive, according to my spiritual principles. I always tried to incorporate what I read in Tolle's books.

We tried going to bed later so that both of us would sleep through the night and not wake up so early. One night we went to bed at midnight. I lay awake until 2:30 a.m. and finally got up to do some work related things. After forty-five minutes, I went back to bed. Around 6:30 a.m., I woke up in the middle of a dream. I had dreamed of visiting my great grandparents, similar to the dream I had had three years ago, before coming to Mexico with John.

In the first dream, my grandfather had remarked, "You aren't in Kansas anymore." Besides the obvious connection for a gay man – Judy Garland, ruby slippers, etc., I had understood it to mean that my life was changing back then, as indeed it was. I had been caught up in my personal tornado!

In the recent dream, we never had a chance to speak. I had been awakened by an outside noise. I so wanted to know what they would say now. And then, I began to have an anxiety attack!

I felt afraid – afraid of going to work that day, afraid of the future with John. I felt so alone. No doubt, all of this had been building as a result of John's anxieties. I stood in the shower, tears flowing. John stepped in and wrapped his arms around me. I attempted to explain what had happened.

On the forty-five minute bus ride into the city, I gave a great deal of thought as to how I had come to this day. With John working nights, I had spent too much time on the chat lines once again, looking for consolation, as well as excitement. Reading Tolle's book, I became very aware that, indeed, my ego was controlling my actions. As long as I allowed that to occur, I wasn't being realistic. I needed to be conscious of what I was doing. The chatting had to stop! With John, I had everything that I was looking for when I had first come 'out' of my closet!!!! One does not find that online.

After work, and with John out teaching, I went to each of the gay web sites I normally visited and deleted all of the so-called 'buddies' I had marked. On MSN Messenger, I deleted all of the contacts except my friends and family.

Having done all of that, I actually did work on the computer related to my job. I wrote a little and read more of Tolle's book. I was being productive again. One day at a time…

***

Subsequently, we both had doctor's appointments in Progreso. On entering her office, together, as we always did, she sensed John's distress. He openly told her what had been going on since his last visit. She suggested something to help him get a good night's sleep and he agreed to try it. Another positive step. She was concerned that he had lost nearly ten pounds since the last visit – another sign of depression.

The first night on the medication, John never woke up once. I, on the other hand, spent most of the night awake, finally falling asleep around 5:30 a.m. When I woke up it was 8:00 a.m.!

I was supposed to be on the bus into the city by then! I hit the floor running and managed to get to work on time...

When I got home from work, we had dinner and then John left for work. While he was out, I made an appointment with our massage guy, Giovanni, to come by and give me one of his excellent massages.

Several weeks passed during which John seemed more like his old persona. We were both still working. I decided that maybe it was time for a 'honey-do" list – one of those lists women do to encourage their spouses to work around the house instead of watching TV all night long. Not that John watched much TV. Indeed, it kept John busy as long as there was a list. He did procrastinate at painting the window grills; I can't say I blamed him. You could paint them and then three or four weeks later, the rust would re-appear, whether you primed them or not. Sand, salt and humidity were the constants in Progreso. No wonder the Maya used only stone and wood...

One day while I was at work, Alberto called. He was our young friend in the city. He needed to talk. I asked him to drop by my work and we chatted for an hour or so. His current love in Mexico City had decided that things were moving too quickly. He needed space. Needless to say, Alberto was devastated – another relationship appearing to crumble. Time for some fatherly words of wisdom. After work, we went to get something to eat. I always wondered if Alberto was eating and sleeping well enough. As we walked down the street, he put his hand on my shoulder. I was surprised – this was a public street. Gay men didn't display affection in public in our part of Mexico...at least not in the daytime! On the other hand, it felt assuring to me. I had told him a little about John and my current problems. It was nice to be able to talk to someone else about it. Just maybe my 'Spirit' had set up this meeting with Alberto to help me, while helping Alberto at the same time. Undoubtedly, I felt that we had the basis of a father-son relationship. I truly believed that he felt the same way.

None too soon, it was time to head back to Canada, albeit only for the four weeks. We'd be seeing family and friends with whom we were no longer that close. Silently, I think both John and I were concerned about the trip.

***

John overcame his bout with depression after the month in Canada. I returned to work in the nearby city and was engrossed in renovations to the building. The fall season was quiet.

Just as the snowbirds began to arrive once again, John and I flew to Mexico City for New Year's Eve as part of a one week tour organized by a Canadian woman and her Mexican husband of over thirty years from the nearby city. Mexico City in January can be very cold! This particular year they had created the world's largest outdoor skating rink in the main *zocalo*...very curious to see Mexicans skating. All of the surrounding government buildings were festooned with

Christmas lights depicting winter figures and Christmas decorations. This IS a Catholic country.

New Year's Eve, we all walked to Garibaldi Park where we were serenaded by the requisite *mariachis*, ever mindful of pickpockets all around. This was followed by dinner at a nearby restaurant where we were entertained by Aztec dancers – scantily clad men and women in traditional costumes, doing fire dances right on the small stage!

At midnight there were real fireworks and sparklers! In my mind were visions of tomorrow's newspaper headlines, "Gringos trapped in blazing restaurant". *'Gringos'* is the term used loosely to describe people from north of the Mexican-US border, a carryover from the Mexican-American war when the soldiers from the north wearing the green uniforms marched into Mexican territory. Thus...green go home...gringo!

During our stay we toured various sights – *the Basilica of Guadalupe*, the Aztec city of T*eotihuacan*, the *National Museum of Anthropology*, the famous floating gardens of *Xochimilco*. Floating down the river on the flower covered boat brought back memories of studying Mexico fifty years earlier when I was a teenager in school. Who would have thought I would be in this place, having made this journey?

Having ignored John's protestations about dressing warmly, I became quite ill with a severe case of bronchitis. Partially to blame was the altitude of Mexico City and its' pollution. Finally, on the morning of our departure, John contacted the hotel doctor, who came and gave me an injection and prescribed several medications. We had no choice but to board the plane later that day for the flight home.

***

We flew home to Progreso and quickly found ourselves in the center of another season of snowbirds. Back were Bobbi and Dick. Most of the flock migrated east of Progreso to another beachside community. There were many new birds in the flock this year, as Mexico and Progreso became increasingly popular as winter destinations for Canadians. The 'gringos' in the nearby city began to refer to Progreso and the nearby beaches as the "Canadian Riviera". The weekly Saturday *hora de feliz* at the neighboring hotel was a sea of unknown faces...

In February 2008, I flew alone to Canada. Unknown to John, and with Ralph's help, I was going to see a divorce lawyer. She was the same lawyer whom both Ralph and Jack had consulted for their respective divorces. I needed to formally end my marriage, having been separated for the last four years. I wanted my wife to be free to move on should the time ever come that she would find someone else with whom to share the rest of her life. I needed to close the door on our marriage, which had taken place forty-two years earlier. How long ago it now seemed!

Upon my return from Canada I informed John of what I had done. On the flight home I had much time to reflect on past, present and future. Now that I was about to be legally divorced, where did I see myself and us headed?

John and I had been together almost four years. Our relationship had grown with time. We knew each other's idiosyncrasies all too well! We had adjusted to living together 24/7 although there had been trials along the way.

We had many straight couples as friends. We never did hang out with a gay crowd or avail ourselves of any of the gay clubs in the city, although we did watch gay porn videos occasionally when we were alone.

Weighing pros and cons, I did love John. I was unsure of whether I could ever be monogamous – especially for the rest of our lives. That weighed heavily on me. My mind once again raced on the airplane returning to Cancun. It continued on the four hour bus ride back to the city where John was waiting at our friend Willie's hotel.

Seven and a half hours after leaving Detroit there I was alone with John. Lying in the bed beside him, I proposed marriage. He accepted without hesitation. With some trepidation, we waited to tell our families and friends while we quietly began to make plans for a wedding back in Canada in the fall of 2008.

***

In July 2008 we joined a gymnasium for some much needed exercise, hoping to get into shape for the wedding.

We both agreed that if Jack was agreeable, we wanted him to perform the ceremony now that he was a licensed minister in Ontario. We wanted our three best friends as witnesses – Jeff, Louise and Ralph. On a trip north, John had checked out a gay owned B and B where Jack and his 'spouse' had been married in 2006. It was near where my daughters and grandchildren lived.

While John was away in Canada I discovered the music of David Freidman after listening to a church service from Detroit. As it turned out, the music had been part of a program of his compositions presented by the Gay Men' Chorus of Washington, D.C. in 2006.

Jack was to be asked to officiate when we traveled north in May. At the same time we would notify our children and close friends in Ontario. We set a September date, giving us time to organize the final plans over the next three months.

Back in Progreso, Jack sent us possible scenarios for the ceremony. We agreed it was best to do our own catering to keep costs down. The guest list was set at about thirty family and friends. We agreed that the B and B would be the venue.

May saw us flying to Ontario and then west to Calgary to visit briefly with our friend Jeff. His *balls* had been dropped here after he had been terminated (near retirement) from his management job in Ontario. We had rented a car at the airport for our drive to British Columbia where we would meet John's oldest son who was working there. We were going to tell him about our forthcoming marriage.

Just prior to leaving Progreso, we had met another Canadian couple in the city. They had spent ten years in Thailand before coming east to Belize to look for a new home. Dissatisfied, they had come over to the nearby city to see if this is where they might live. They wanted to be closer to their families in Canada. They were undecided about whether to locate in the city or at the beach.

On the spur of the moment, we rented them our house for the next month since it was going to be vacant anyways. Four days later we left! Talk about trust!

When we returned at the end of the month, they had fallen in love with Progreso and rented another place for six months to give themselves time to scout out properties. They ended up buying a home just two blocks from us! The Canadian flock just kept growing!

****

I had never been further west than Sault Ste. Marie, Ontario. I had seen the Rockies when I had travelled to California, but never up close and personal. They were majestic! I was inspired to write a few poems commenting on the trip.

We crossed over to Vancouver Island where we spent some time with old friends of John's whom he had known since childhood. In Campbell River we gathered fresh oysters for a beachside BBQ.

All too soon, I had to return to Progreso. John flew back to Ontario to sell his Toyota before returning to Mexico. We had decided that it was time to buy a car in Mexico with Mexican plates to avoid any potential problems with the police, like those we had had previously in Mexico City.

From then on it was a whirlwind of activity as we scrambled to make the final arrangements for the early September wedding. We agreed on the order of service, the music, the receptions, and the guest list. John's youngest son would attend, although the oldest could not since he was in British Columbia still. My ex-wife and her friend were invited but declined so as not to impact on "our" day as she put it. (She did send us a great greeting card). John and I wrote our own vows unknown to each other or the minister, Jack.

Initially, my oldest daughter was reluctant to commit even though we had chosen a date that was free for her to attend! Our thinking was, "How could she explain grandpa's wedding to her young children?" My youngest daughter had concerns about how my oldest granddaughter would handle this. When we left for Canada in early September we were still not sure of either's attendance. I was hopeful.

In Canada, we had very little time to organize the wedding and the reception. Day One was occupied getting the license. We decided to have a pre-reception so our families and friends could meet, followed by the actual ceremony, followed by a celebratory reception where we served our "*21 carat cake*" (Costco) and wine. John and I both loved carrot cake!

On the day of the wedding, both of my daughters and their families attended. We had three ministers – Jack and two friends who were also ministers in the US, one of whom was Cristina. Jack was the official minister for our wedding.

My eldest granddaughter was our official photographer. The day was warm for September. Our guests arrived an hour before the actual ceremony and enjoyed the appetizers which we had prepared ourselves, along with a fruit punch and wine.

Minutes before the ceremony, John and I disappeared for one last quiet moment, while *David Freidman's* "My White Knight" played in the background. We had chosen the song as it was about a stranger coming into town in a pickup truck and meeting the love of *his* life! Jack had a pickup truck when I first met him, so it was very appropriate. When that song ended, John and I reappeared. When it came time we read our respective vows in public for the first time. Both of us were a little emotional at that point. At the end we had our rings blessed and were pronounced "partners in life". We celebrated with champagne and that 21 carrot cake…

Following the wedding we headed east to visit John's friends near Toronto. They surprised us with a small reception at a local restaurant. We visited John's former mother-in-law and her sister east of Toronto.

Within the week we returned to Progreso where our Regina friends, Tim and Suzanne, hosted a reception/pool party for our beach friends. To be economical, we excluded our city friends at this time. That reception would be held later when more of the snowbirds had arrived. Our life began as a married couple!

We had first met Tim and Suzanne while walking one night in Progreso in 2007. They had arrived to investigate properties where they could operate a small bed without breakfast operation. Too young to retire, Tim was operating an online Internet business in Canada. Suzanne was a lab technician back in Regina.

After buying their property, five blocks from us, they returned to Regina, selling their Canadian home very quickly. Within four months, they were residents of Progreso.

It was not long after this, that another couple from the Midwest United States became residents of Progreso too!

Our circle of friends just kept getting bigger...

***

In November, our friends from California, Donna and Carl, who had recently completed remodeled their city home, hosted a reception in our honor for ninety-five people. John and I decided to share the day with another gay couple who had recently moved here from California. They had been married in California *twice* because of the changes in the laws there. It was our way of introducing the two women to many of our friends. Eighty-five percent of the guests were straight couples! In attendance were Tom and Frank, Francisco and Gloria, Alberto, Willie and his wife and son, and Tim and Suzanne, from Regina. There were many others whose *balls* had been dropped in the Yucatan long before we arrived in 2004...

It was catered by our gay Italian friend, Angelo. Yes, we had handsome young waiters and another gay friend as the bartender. Towards the end of the evening, our hostess made a very impassioned speech about changing times (Obama had been elected as the first Black President of the United States) and gay marriages. All in attendance listened appreciatively. Some of our straight friends had tears in their eyes as she read from her prepared text.

***

Our landlords continued to get along like the proverbial cats and dogs. Gloria spent a lot of time at her oldest daughter's restaurant in Playa Del Carmen, before it was sold for lack of business. After two years of marriage, no grandchildren were forthcoming, much to Gloria's disappointment.

Francisco's youngest daughter had previously found a new boyfriend; he was from England and had come to the Yucatan to study Spanish. In January 2009 she flew to Rome to visit the sister of her Italian brother-in-law whom she had met when her sister got married. The flight was paid for by her sister, her mother and her brother, Tomas. Francisco was not happy when he found out about the planned trip. He refused to give her any money! Moments before her departure from Cancun, he showed up at the airport to see her off.

From Rome, she went to Spain with her English boyfriend. He was now studying near Barcelona. Francisco was not happy to learn that they were sharing an apartment while there. They travelled to Paris and then to England to see his family before returning to Spain. While she was travelling, events back home in Progreso took a bad turn…

In early February, after our return once again from Canada, Francisco underwent a colonoscopy. Two days later he was admitted to hospital with extreme abdominal pain. His blood pressure dropped to the point where they were afraid to do the necessary surgery. The family felt it necessary to move him to another hospital, fearing he would not survive. Forty-five minutes after being admitted, Francisco underwent reconstructive bowel surgery. The poison had spread throughout his body. The doctors gave him a twenty percent chance of survival.

He would spend almost two weeks in the private hospital in Intensive Care. His family maintained vigilance at his bedside. He was given a complete colostomy to drain the fluids. Within two days of the first surgery he underwent a second for a hernia repair.

Unfortunately for Francisco, he was uninsured for his stay and surgery in the private hospital! The resultant bill was almost 100,000 pesos – more than three times his annual teaching salary!

When he was well enough, he was moved to a public hospital where he was covered. He was discharged and spent another month living with his wife's niece in the nearby city so that his doctor could visit every night and check on him. He finally returned to Progreso on Good Friday. He had been resurrected! It would be some time before he could return to work again.

The cloud of a 100,000 peso debt hung over his head. John and I organized a benefit breakfast at a restaurant run by one of Francisco's friends. We anticipated donations of ten to twelve thousand pesos. We ended up with thirty thousand pesos – most of it from our Canadian and American friends. Unable to attend, Francisco sent Tomas to deliver a speech on his behalf. He had been humbled by the generosity and love of so many strangers!!! We were very proud of our friends too.

***

In February of 2009, we embarked on a group trip to Puebla and Oaxaca. Many of those on the trip we had met on our previous trip to Mexico City. Most were Americans.

We flew to Mexico City and then boarded a private bus for Puebla, well-known as the Mexican headquarters of Volkswagen. We were fortunate to stay in a hotel right on the main square. Each day we would set off on trips to nearby sites – cathedrals, museums, etc. dining each night at a different outdoor restaurant under the stars. How romantic!

Leaving Puebla, we took the bus again, heading for Oaxaca. En route, John became ill. The moment we checked into the new hotel, we summoned a doctor. We were relieved when he arrived very quickly. He also spoke English, and we later learned that he had trained in North Carolina. John was diagnosed with severe bronchitis. The doctor checked me over as well. Within less than half an hour, John was on medication. The doctor left, giving us his personal cellphone number should John's condition change during the night. In Mexico, doctors do make house calls and give you their private cell phone numbers!

The next morning, with John seeming better, we walked to the nearby cathedral. John became easily exhausted and we returned to the hotel to rest. With John sleeping quietly, I went for a walk to further explore the city. Later, the doctor came by to check on John's progress.

The following day, the group was to tour nearby *Monte Alban*, another historical site. I insisted that John stay put for the day and I chose to stay behind and keep an eye on him. The following day he was still not up to par. He insisted that I go with the group on another tour. By the time we got back, John was feeling well enough to go out for dinner.

As we were leaving Oaxaca the next day, John received a phone call from the doctor, again checking on his condition, which was now greatly improved!

We bussed back to Mexico City, and boarded our plane for the return trip to Progreso. En route, I texted our local doctor to bring her up to speed on what had transpired with John. As soon as we were back, she came by the house to check on him. She prescribed some additional medications.

***

One week later, my older sister and her husband came to visit from Canada. I was apprehensive, as we had never really spent much time together before my mother had died. Interestingly, we had begun to communicate regularly via the Internet after the funeral. We had a great time with them, but unfortunately, the moment they left John became ill again.

The doctor came by and made arrangements for John to be hospitalized for further treatment of the recurring bronchitis. I was stunned when she showed up at the hospital at nine o'clock at night to check on him! The hospital was a forty minute drive from her home...

The more time we spent in Progreso, the more we were impressed by the doctors and the Mexican medical system.

***

The next month we had more visitors from Canada – a classmate of John's from university and his wife. By now we had visited the Maya ruins at Uxmal so many times that we could practically conduct the tour without a guide! It was and still is our favorite place to take visitors AND it was near our friend's restaurant, allowing us to have lunch after the tour.

After Easter we went on a long weekend trip to *Rio Logartos* (east of us) and north of the well-known ruins/modern Wonder of the World – Chichen Itza. On the way we also visited *Ek Balam*.

Rio Logartos is best known for its ecotourism. We travelled by boat along the waterways, snapping photos of all types of birds and water animals. At the turn around point, we all got out and covered our faces and arms in mud, part of a ritual handed down from the Maya. It is said to have medicinal benefits! The clay dried on us as we motored back.

After dropping off the other two guests, our guide took us to a secluded beach where we could strip naked and rinse off the dried clay, while he waited for us. It was quite the experience!

Summers in Progreso are not necessarily pleasurable. Besides the heat, our little town of 25,000 grows to 100,000 with the influx of the nearby city dwellers who escape the city heat. It sometimes appears as if every city resident owns a beachfront home or condo, or rents a place in the town for the six weeks of the *temporada.*

Cars line the highway from the city, heading north to the beach. When we first arrived there was a two lane road. That has subsequently been changed to six lanes! Streets and stores become very crowded. Restaurants in the city close temporarily and open beach locations. Some even offer valet parking!

It is a raucous time with crowded beaches and fiestas many days each week. By comparison, *Semana Santa* lasts only two weeks. Every house on our street is occupied. Of course, there is an increase of garbage and vehicles.

While we are very busy socially during the winter months with our snowbird friends, summer often finds us in the city with other friends who live here year round. We would also normally spend a few weeks each summer in Canada. As summer was a slow time at my work, I could easily get away for a few weeks. The rest of the year I was kept very busy with a variety of events.

It was in 2009 that I completed my second book and had it published. It had been my goal to complete 100 poems by the end of 2008. It was close. The last one was done in January. The title, which I had original planned to be "In Spirit's Time", was changed to "Trust the

Winds", the title of a song we played at our wedding in September 2008. The cover of the book displayed a photograph I had taken while visiting John's son in Nelson, British Columbia.

That fall, we launched the book with about thirty friends at the home of our California friends, Connie and Sheila. As was the norm, John read the poems after they were briefly introduced by me. He always enjoyed reading my poetry out loud. I never ceased to be amazed by how my words were internalized by various listeners. On some occasions, in our home, I had seen tears in their eyes. They were as touched as I was.

***

In February 2010 we set off with a small group of expat friends to once again travel to Palenque, Yaxchilan and Bonampak. The idea was to take our cameras and receive instruction on how to make the nest use of them at the various locations. Our guide was an excellent photographer. He was the son of one of our close friends whom we had come to know a few years after we arrived in Progreso.

Her '*balls*' had been dropped in the Yucatan thirty years ago, when as a travel professional, she brought a group of Canadians here on a vacation. Her Mexican tour guide was a young lawyer with whom she fell in love almost immediately. Six months later they were married in Canada! (Our tour guide was their oldest son).

At our first stop in Palenque, we contacted a previous site guide, Francisco, who took us into the jungle, not normally seen by first time visitors. We were accompanied by two women friends, one Mexican, the other American. Our guide introduced us to jungle cuisine...live termites, fresh from the nest! Que sorpresa! They tasted like carrots. They were certainly better than the *chapulines* (grasshoppers) we had tasted in Oaxaca on our previous trip. Back at the hotel we regaled our friends with this experience.

Rising very early the following day, we travelled to Yaxchilan, taking a *lancha* to the site as we had done before. Yaxchilan is the only Maya site accessible by water only. It nestles beside the Usumacinta River across from Guatemala. After lunch we headed back to Bonampak to spend the night.

Imagine our surprise when we pulled into a farmyard a few kilometers from the gates of Bonampak. We would be spending the night in a converted chicken coup with concrete floors, half walls between the rooms and an outdoor shower and bathrooms! Men and women slept in separate complexes. Fortunately, the chickens were roaming outside along with the other farm animals. To further add to the ambiance, the restaurant served NO BEER or alcohol. This particular night they had also run out of bottled water!!! We were pleased when our van driver offered to go to a nearby village where he could buy both beer and water.

Surprisingly, we had one of the best meals of the trip in the restaurant, even though there were less chickens walking around that night…

Morning saw us head off to Bonampak, and then returning to Palenque to our previous hotel for one last night. Indeed, it was a memorable trip!

***

As soon as we returned to Progreso, we began making plans for another trip to Europe. John had decided that we would celebrate my sixty-fifth birthday and that this would be his gift to me. We began to scour the Internet sites and the familiar gay website for accommodations and places to visit. This was the same time when the Iceland volcano chose to erupt!

Ultimately, we decided to fly into Rome where we would spend three days, and then take a train to Cinque Terre, followed by flights to Paris and Prague. From Prague we booked a train to Budapest. In Budapest, we elected to book a one week Danube River cruise east to Vienna and on to Nuremberg. After Nuremberg, we had two weeks to spend between Cologne, Brugges and Amsterdam. We allowed ourselves six weeks of travel in all, as I was still working …

With the itinerary and travel plans out of the way, we proceeded to look for the accommodations and to book tours in each city. Indeed this would be the trip of a lifetime for two Canadian farm boys! Walking down the dark country roads fifty years ago, looking up at the stars, I could never have imagined that my *"balls"* would be travelling across the Atlantic Ocean not once, but twice...

We decided that we would leave near the end of April and return in early June. Thoughts of April in Paris entered my mind. Three months before our departure, we were allowed to post our itinerary on the gay website again. What followed were various invitations offering accommodations, tour guides and more...

We carefully examined the offers of accommodation. When there were no offers in some cities, John searched the Internet. As it turned out, we accepted offers in Rome, Prague and Budapest. John found other B and B's in Cinque Terre, Paris, Cologne, Brugges and Amsterdam.

We also were able to chat with men in all of the cities, picking their brains as to where to go, what to see, etc. In some instances we webcammed with the guys.

John wanted this to be a trip with no regrets. He wanted us to see and do, just in case we would never have the opportunity again. And so it was to be...

***

Utilizing the gay resources, we rented a small apartment on the ground floor in Rome near the Colosseum. It was one of two owned by a gay couple – one Italian, the other from Argentina who also lived in the building in another very small apartment. There was a double bed, a closet, a kitchen sink, washing machine and a small bathroom with a shower. At less than 500 square feet it was to be our smallest accommodation of the trip. The guys seemed nice enough and we went out together to a neighborhood bistro for dinner. We didn't really see them much during the day.

Since we had been in Rome previously, we chose to check out lesser known attractions this time – church basements, caverns dating back hundreds of years (catacombs), the *Appian Way*, *Hadrian's Villa* and *Tivoli*. We did do two tours with the same company we had used in 2006. As our previous guide, Thomas, was otherwise occupied, he introduced us to another friend for those tours. He told us about a great restaurant across the river in Trastavere, where we lunched on calamari and grilled asparagus... very good indeed.

We had arranged to meet Thomas to go wine bar hopping one night after he was done work. This turned out to be the highlight of our visit. We managed only two bars in the pouring rain – one near the Forum, the other in Trastavere. Thomas picked one while I picked the other.

Being inventive gay guys, we agreed to order three different wines at the first bar and we passed our glasses amongst ourselves while Thomas took tasting notes. We then moved on to the next bar, an "*enoteca*" the Italian word for wine bar.

The *Enoteca Ferrara* is located on the island of Trastavere across the Tiber River from Rome.

Upon entry, your attention focuses on the wall of wine barrels and spigots. Below the barrels are actual bottles of the wines and a chalkboard showing prices by glass, bottle or carafe! We made our choices from three different price ranges – the most expensive was 80 euros! As before, we purchased only red wines, took our seats on low stools in the corner and shared them! To satiate our appetites, we ordered a cheese and meat platter with lots of fresh Italian breads. In the pouring rain, the three of us hopped in a taxi and headed back into Rome, leaving Thomas to return to his apartment. Two days later, we boarded our train to Vernazza in the Cinque Terre.

***

The *Cinque Terre* is a rugged portion of coast on the Italian Riviera. It is in the Liguria region of Italy, to the west of the city of La Spezia. "The Five Lands" is composed of five villages: Monterosso al Mare, Vernazza, Corniglia, Manarola, and Riomaggiore. The coastline, the five villages, and the surrounding hillsides are all part of the Cinque Terre National Park and are a UNESCO World Heritage Site.

Over the centuries, people have carefully built terraces on the rugged, steep landscape right up to the cliffs that overlook the sea. Part of its charm is the lack of visible corporate development. Paths, trains and boats connect the villages, and cars cannot reach them from the outside. The Cinque Terre area is a very popular tourist destination.

(The villages of the Cinque Terre were severely affected by torrential rains which caused floods and mudslides on October 25, 2011. Nine people were confirmed killed by the floods, and damage to the villages, particularly Vernazza and Monterosso al Mare, was extensive).

Arriving in Vernazza by train, we walked under the tunnel into the town. We had reserved a room in a private home with an older Italian lady who spoke no English. We were shown to our room which overlooked the narrow sidewalk surrounded on each side by more houses. Clotheslines across the streets joined the quaint houses while townspeople strolled below.

After a couple of Proseccos and biscotti on her terrace we headed down to the sea. We were surrounded by vineyards to the east and the Tyrrhenian Sea to the east. The panorama was awesome in all directions. The hillsides are covered by grape terraces, accessible by climbing steep steps branching out from the many trails. Of course, fishing is also important here. The anchovies were incredible!

From Vernazza the trails go in two directions. To the south Corniglia, Manarola and Riomaggiore; to the north is Monterosso al Mare.

Day two we set off early on the trail south to Riomaggiore. Along the way we stopped at Manarola, sipping a great Sicilian wine, nibbling on cheese, salami and Italian bread fresh from the oven. It had taken us three hours to walk here. Too tired to walk further we took a boat back to Vernazza. Dinner that night was at a small sidewalk café, feasting on white wine, calamari and olives, of course.

The next morning we headed up the hill to Il Pirata – a restaurant owned by two Sicilian brothers who carried on like the Smothers Brothers of the 60's. They constantly bantered with each other and their customers in English and Italian. Besides being a great bakery, they had excellent breakfasts. We would go there in the evenings for dinner also.

Our next trek took us to Monterosso al Mare. We could clearly see the train tracks which linked the five towns.

It was a very romantic time for us, walking the trail, sipping wine overlooking the sea, under the starlit skies at night. Too soon we had to return to Pisa to catch our flight to Paris! Our stopover in Pisa was brief – not even enough time to actually visit the Leaning Tower, but we could see it from the train as we approached from the north.

***

I was pretty confident about the French leg of our trip since I knew John would have no problem communicating in French. What they say about Paris in springtime was not true! It was cold and rainy as we arrived. Where we really in London? Nope...we took the Metro from Orly to our apartment five blocks from *Notre Dame Cathedral.* We were met by a friend of the English owners who gave us the keys and showed us the unit (slightly larger than Rome) on the fifth floor. It did have a very small elevator which we had to use one at a time.

Unpacking again, we decided to shop for a few groceries, have dinner in and relax before the very full days ahead. We also purchased scarves and gloves to stay warm! We made full use of the electric heat that night.

In the morning, we started the rigorous task of seeing as much as we could of Paris in one week. This day included a visit to *Cluny Museum*, Notre Dame Cathedral, *Sainte Chapelle*, crossing the Seine on Pont Neuf. In the afternoon, we strolled through *Luxembourg Gardens*, then the *Rodin Museum*, crossing *Pont de la Concorde* and then back to the apartment.

We rose early the next morning to buy tickets to a Vivaldi concert at Ste. Chapelle, and then took the Metro to the *Eiffel Tower*, stopping to buy tickets for a Fat Tire Bike Tour of Versailles the next morning. Due to the high winds, the Eiffel was closed! We walked instead to the *Arc de Triomphe*...closed for renovations! Double whammy...

Walking the Champs d'Elysee, we stopped for lunch at the famous *Fouquet's* where I experience my first ever Croque Monsieur (grilled cheese sandwich) – 36 Euros!!! After lunch we explored the gardens of *Tuileries* and the *Louvre*. In the evening we attended the concert at Ste. Chapelle. Seeing it in the evening was even more impressive than the daytime. Every wall is a mass of stained glass windows.

The acoustics were incredible. It was so breathtaking.

Arising early Sunday, we took the Metro to the office of Fat Tire Bike Tours. Each of our group picked out a bicycle and took a short spin before joining our tour leaders on a short ride to the train station. After boarding and securing our bikes, we departed for the town of Versailles.

Pedaling into the town center from the station, we stopped at the market and purchased food and wine for our picnic on the grounds of the Place – cheese, fresh bread, cold meats, strawberries, some pate and lots of wine, of course!

We rode into the Palace grounds, stopping for a brief orientation by our tour guides at Marie Antoinette's farm as we circled the lake. Just as we were about half way around, it started to hail! Yes, HAIL!!! So much for April in Paris, *Doris Day!!*

We concluded the bike tour at the Palace, where we had expected to see the famous fountain show (as well as the Hall of Mirrors). Unfortunately the rain continued...

Qué sera sera....we headed back to town and the rail station before going directly back to our apartment...high and dry!

We toured the Louvre for two hours the next morning, fighting our way through the mass of tourists to get a glimpse of the *Mona Lisa*. So disappointing that she is secured behind a glass panel preventing any good photo!!! Tiring of the crowds, we headed to see Monet's 'Water Lilies' at the *Orangerie*.

Getting out of the rain meant going shopping at the very well known *Galeries Lafayette*, no doubt the most expensive and beautiful shopping mall that I have ever seen.

That same night we were joined at dinner by a couple whom we met on the bike tour. Their *'balls'* had been dropped in Paris after a long delayed flight from Southern California.

What followed was a recommended Paris Floodlit Tour by taxi, as recommended in a Rick Steve's tour book. We found a driver who was very familiar with the route we wanted to take. He knew exactly the spots to stop at to get the best photos. It was a memorable night. We ended the night with Mexican 'churros' in the Trocadero.

Five hours were spent the following day at the *Orsay Museum* – Paris' former train station. We both agreed that it was much more spectacular than the staid Louvre, with the dour Mona Lisa.

En route back to the apartment and our last dinner in Paris we stopped and paid our respects to Napoleon, whose *'balls'* were dropped there after the Revolution. The next afternoon we flew from Charles de Gaulle Airport on to our next stop in the Czech Republic – Prague.

***

Arriving in Prague by air at 4 pm we were whisked away by limousine to our apartment steps from Wenceslas Square. This apartment was a result of a search on the gay website also. It was one of two in the building that the two gay owners rented out. The furnishings were all from the department store, IKEA. Amazingly, we rented it for 400 euros, including the limo service!

We awoke the next morning with John being sick...not an auspicious start to the week ahead!

By noon he was feeling better and we headed off, camera in hand, to capture this incredible city in photos. Around every corner were wonderful buildings with amazing architecture and frescoes. The buildings in Prague were not affected by any wars over the years.

We were to attend a concert by the Czech Philharmonic Orchestra, but it was cancelled at the last minute as a result of the director being fired that same morning by the Minister of Culture. The orchestra simply refused to play, much to the anger of the Czechs in attendance.

The following day our serious sightseeing began – *Old Town*, the historical *Astronomical Clock*, *St. Vitus Cathedral*, the Royal Gardens, the *Charles Bridge*, *Mala Strena*, the *Powder Gate*, *Jewish Quarter* and a cruise on the Vtala River. Six hours later we returned to our apartment.

We had met Leo, an American gay, online before we left for Europe. He had been teaching English to Czech businessmen for several years. Like us, he had been married and had children in

Atlanta. He was picking up the pieces of his life in this wonderful city. Indeed, it was he who introduced us to the owners of our apartment, one of whom had been his young lover at some point in time.

Ending the day, we went to dinner with Leo at a wonderful French restaurant across the river, agreeing to meet the next morning to take the train to *Karlstjein Castle* with him. We had a great time at the Castle that day and also got to see more of the Czech countryside.

The rains started again…our *'balls'* were getting waterlogged in Europe! When it finally stopped the next morning we continued to explore. Taking more photos – *Kafka House*, Grand Praha Hotel, the Cathedral, stopping to buy tickets to a Gershwin concert being held at the *Spanish Synagogue* the next evening. We had only two nights left before we would take the train to Budapest – our next stop. Our final days were spent walking, walking and walking. We were falling in love with Prague!

***

When we had registered our itinerary on the gay website, it was from Budapest that we got the most responses – all kinds of 'offers'; there was one offer of accommodation that caught our eyes – a 38 year old gay Hungarian who offered us an apartment or the second bedroom in his apartment. After chatting online we accepted the latter offer…38 euros per night!

Walking from the Budapest train station, we easily found his apartment and walked up the five flights of stairs with our luggage – a little detail he left out! Our host was a handsome six foot tall, young man who showed us to our bedroom on the second floor of his own apartment, complete with a private terrace overlooking Budapest! We had certainly lucked out with this connection in more ways than we had expected. Needing to get some Hungarian money we walked to a nearby bank and then stopped for lunch at a typical Hungarian restaurant, enjoying 'gulas' and a cold Pilsner beer.

The other connection we had made was with a gay massage therapist in Budapest. As it turned out, he was a friend of our host and lived just a few blocks away. As our host was going out for the evening with other friends, we asked if he minded if we invited the therapist over to give us massages after the long train ride. He had no problem with that, and so we came to meet Zoldt a few hours later. Indeed, he was a trained massage therapist who gave us both great massages before leaving. We hoped we could have another massage before we left Budapest, but there was not enough time.

Early the next morning we set out on a walking tour of Budapest. Our host had been born there and offered his services as our guide for the day. That was another reason we had connected with him. What a tour we had! We started at 8 a.m. sharp and headed off for breakfast at a little stand near the zoo. After that we began what turned out to be a fourteen hour marathon tour of Budapest on foot, by subway, and by bus.

First stop – the famous *Széchenyi Baths*, world renown. As it was still quite early, we didn't partake, but looked around. We then boarded the subway and headed to the area near the Hungarian Parliament. This was followed by a trip to see the US Embassy, the Community Monument, *St. Stephen's Cathedral* and *Gresham Palace*. *Buda Castle* was our next stop across the river, travelling over the famous Chain Bridge. Again it started to rain… Changing plans we headed back to the same wonderful restaurant near our host's apartment and lunched on Hungarian Goulash once again. By this time a rest was in order…

According to our host, the day was still young. Were we interested in a Turkish bath? When in Rome, er Budapest – of course we were! As it turned out it was men's day at the oldest of the baths in Budapest – *Rudas*. That was certainly all that was needed to convince these two gay guys.

In spite of the obvious language barrier, we had our host put us through the rigors of the baths – warm water, cold water, hot water, all the while surrounded by naked men of all ages. I should point out, that upon admission one is given a *small* paper jockstrap which quickly deteriorates when wet!

Prior to the ritual we each had a wet massage, alternating hot and cold water poured over your naked body, with frequent massaging in between.

Finally we got to use the five swimming pools, each one slightly hotter than the previous one. I will make no further comments, except to say we would never have considered this without our gracious host! We would never have had the '*balls*' to do this.

When we finally finished at the baths we walked across the Chain Bridge to continue our tour. We reached the apartment at 10 p.m.....very tired!

The next morning we walked around the central area, exploring various museums and markets. We returned to the apartment to say our goodbyes and thanks, picking up our luggage. A taxi took us to our waiting cruise ship on the Danube River – one last night before we would set sail towards Vienna and six nights along the way to Germany.

***

For the next seven days our '*balls*' would be cruising on the Danube River between Budapest and Regensburg, Germany, along with approximately 140 other tourists, mostly Americans. The first night was great, watching a wonderful thunder and lightening storm over Buda Castle, from the ship's lounge. We departed on schedule at 8 a.m. the next morning.

Seeming to be two single men, we connected in the bar with two seemingly single women – both from an island off the coast of England. Actually, both turned out to be married, but were vacationing without their husbands on this trip.

There was an almost immediate bond, which continued to evolve during the cruise. They knew we were gay, but we came to spend the week in their constant company. Of course, we talked about each other's lives, our families, previous trips, etc. over countless drinks and many bottles of wine. We laughed a lot. The older lady loved to dance which John was more than willing to do. The younger lady and I sat and chatted endlessly. She was actually the age of my oldest daughter back in Canada.

As we sipped our drinks that first night a huge storm blanketed Budapest as I previously mentioned. Buda Castle looked so ominous. Indeed, it was a dark and stormy night, but the four of us had a great time listening to the band and chatting as we watched the older people trotting off to bed.....Indeed, almost every night we were the last ones to leave the lounge. Usually we had a last drink with the piano player and the bar staff before calling it a night.

Our multinational crew was great in every way. They were so accommodating to our every request. The cruise director was Romanian. The hotel manager was German. The bar staff were Hungarian and Czech. We got to know the latter quite well during our seven days since John had purchased a premium bar package for us.

"Kahlua with your coffee this morning, sirs?"

When we decried the fact that there was no limoncello aboard, our bartender got off the ship at the first stop and bought two bottles. They were reserved for us only! Another day we purchased cold cuts, cheese and olives and the bartender kept them in the bar fridge for us to enjoy in the evening when we returned from our shore tours.

After breakfast on the third day we arrived in Vienna. We were only there for twelve hours, so we had planned ahead and booked dinner and a concert at *Schönbrunn Palace*.

Disembarking the ship we went on a group tour of the city's sights by bus, taking in the *Rinstrasse*, *Opera House*, *Stadtpark*, and *Hofsburg Theater* before stopping at *St. Stephen's Cathedral*. Many of us chose to shop along the pedestrian Kartnerstrasse before heading for the Hofsburg Palace, winter home of the family.

Our next Metro trip took us out to Schönbrunn Palace where we toured the grounds and gardens teeming with sculptures and trees, ponds and waterfalls. Eventually it was time for dinner in the Orangerie of the Palace.

It was finally time for the long awaited concert in this "City of Waltzes". Unfortunately, it had been relocated from the Palace into a much less elegant building due to renovations underway in the Great Hall. Nevertheless, it was memorable hearing the Blue Danube Waltz performed by the Vienna Orchestra in the *Orangerie* of the Palace.

Scurrying to the subway, we returned to the ship to enjoy another late evening with the ladies, sipping our limoncello and dancing as we set sail for our next stop.

Our second stop on the trip was to be to the west of Bratislava, a town called Melk. It was the site of a huge *Benedictine Abbey.* You have to understand that John and I are very spiritual. Churches of any type are unimpressive to us no matter how grand they are in size or décor. Melk was indeed massive as we could clearly see as we approached from the East. One could only wonder what the people of the day thought of the elaborate Baroque architectural gem? From the courtyards to the terraces with their view of the Wachau Valley, to the extensive library with its collection of medieval manuscripts, we had to admit that this one was impressive nevertheless.

Completing the tour of the Abbey, we strolled through the little town before heading back to the ship. The rest of the day and evening was onboard, as we continued to get to know some of the other passengers. It appeared that we were the only gay couple, a fact we didn't hide from anyone.

After dinner everyone headed to the lounge to enjoy some more music and drinks. Lots of couples were up dancing, including my spouse and one of our lady friends. On the spur of the moment, and with the pianist playing a slow song, I stepped up and asked John to dance! I knew he would not say "No". He loves to dance. It was so uncharacteristic of me to dance with him in public in Canada or Mexico. Then again, at the end of the seven days we'd never see any of these people again. What did we care?

A few dances later we returned to our drinks to the congratulations of some of our fellow passengers. One lady in particular took the time to tell us how happy we had made her. She explained that she had a lesbian daughter and always worried about how she would be accepted in public with her partner. We had opened her eyes by our actions. I guess that was another reason why our *'balls'* had been dropped on this cruise.

The next morning after breakfast we disembarked in Passau, walking its narrow streets to *Oberhaus Fortress* through the Old Town to *St. Stephen's Cathedral* (yes, another St. Stephen's) where we were treated to a special concert played on the 17000 pipe organ, considered Europe's largest. It was indeed special – even though no one could recognize the piece being played!

We skipped lunch and toured around the town, returning to the ship for afternoon drinks and getting ready for dinner that evening.

Sailing through the night, we awoke in Regensburg, Germany. Of all of the places we had visited, aside from Vienna, this was our favourite on the cruise.

After a brief walking tour, we were on our own to explore the 13th century town – one of Europe's best preserved medieval towns, and no St. Stephen's! Okay, there was a St. Peter's, the home church of then Pope Benedict's brother…miraculously now undergoing extensive renovations since his rise to the Papacy!

Finding a quaint spot at the foot of the bridge, we seated ourselves at a wooden picnic table and dined on bratwurst and sauerkraut a la fresco (I know that's not German), washed down with very cold German beer.

We had no choice but to walk that off by doing some Christmas shopping in the center of town, ending the stop in this wonderful town with some exquisite chocolate and handmade Christmas decorations.

In the afternoon we opted for a Danube Narrows excursion, travelling by road to Kelheim and then boarding a ferry to explore the cliffs and dramatic scenery of *Weltenburg Abbey*, renowned for its dark ale brewed by monks since 1050.

We rejoined the ship near Kelheim just before dinner – at the Captain's Table!

I neglected to say that my spouse and I, along with our two lady friends had been invited to sit at the Captain's Table for the final night's dinner. Since the ship's captain spoke only Russian, he seconded the hotel manager to do the honors this night. The four of us had befriended the manager throughout the trip. When asked by other guests how we rated such an honor we responded in unison, "We slept with the captain!"

We had an incredible dinner with unlimited wines and liqueurs. It was memorable…

On our last day at sea we travelled through a number of locks comprising the Mein-Danube Canal – 106 miles from Bamburg to Kelheim on the Danube River. It was started in 793 but not completed until 1992 – 16 locks that raise the water level 1332 feet! Our final shore excursion saw us visiting the *Nazi Parade grounds* in Nuremberg, and the *Documentation Center Museum*, prior to exploring Old Town and the wonderful market square with its elaborate Gothic drinking fountain.

The time had come to disembark the ship which had brought us so many wonderful memories and so many new friends. Saying goodbye to our two lady friends was very hard and somewhat emotional for all of us. Not looking back we grabbed our bags and walked to the train station and headed for our next stop, Cologne, Germany.

***

We had not expected the station to be so close to the incredible Cathedral, which we both agreed surpassed any we had seen on this trip! We walked around and stopped for coffee and pastry at a small outdoor restaurant right across from the Cathedral. This would not be our last time there.

Our days here were idyllic – touring the city on a double decker bus, crossing the Rhine River on a cable car, dining out and walking everywhere.

Two days later we boarded the train again for Brussels, ending up in Brugges – known as the

"Venice of the North" due to its large numbers of canals. The buildings were very picturesque, reflecting their Gothic origins. Our B and B was situated on one such canal. Inside there was an abundance of original art covering the walls, literally…no frames and painted directly on the wall.

Brugges is known for mussels due to its proximity to the sea. They were our first meal, washed down with local Belgian beer – *De Halve Maan*. We actually toured the brewery one day and ended up going back for more beer more than once. Imagine, gay guys not drinking wine? The accompanying *waterzooi* – fish stew was excellent as well!

Another day we borrowed our hostess' bicycles and went exploring along the canals north of the city getting our first real view of windmills. Every canal side village had at least one!

One evening we met up with a gay guy we had met online before the trip. His home was within walking distance of our B and B as it turned out. He invited us over for dinner. We were not aware that he worked for a major seaside hotel. He prepared us a wonderful meal of shrimp with fresh herbs from his garden. Completing the foursome at dinner, he had also invited a friend to come out from Brussels – a very handsome guy.

We had pre-arranged a day trip to the battlefields/cemeteries of WW I and II in Flanders, exploring the countryside along the way. I particularly wanted to see the Vancouver epitaph which marked the place where my grandfather had been gassed during WW I. I left a message in the visitor's log along with a red poppy (conveniently supplied by one of our fellow travelers that day). Thousands of young Canadians lost their lives in this area. Later, we stopped by Essex, the site of a marker honoring John McCrae who wrote "*In Flanders Fields*".

Each morning at the B and B we had breakfast with a young German woman from Cologne. As it turned out she was a closeted lesbian. We spent a lot of time with her, with my spouse trying out his old German from his childhood – 45 years earlier. When we ultimately left Brugges for Amsterdam she insisted on carrying our luggage to the train station and waited until our train departed. To this day we are still in touch.

The train ride from Brugges through Brussels to Amsterdam seemed to pass quickly. Once again we had pre-booked a B and B not far from the train station and *very* close to the Red Light district and the gay neighborhood. Our third floor room with bath overlooked a canal from which tourist ferries departed.

From there we could walk to most places and/or take a streetcar. Long days were spent visiting with Rembrandt, eating Indonesian food, touring the *Rijksmuseum*, etc. Of course we did a canal tour and also visited Anne Frank's family home.

One day our friend from Leewaurden drove down and picked us up at the train station. We drove out over the Zuider Zee, stopping for lunch at the very picturesque town of Sloten. All along the roadways were corrals of Friesian horses, and more windmills. After touring his hometown, we returned to the train station for our trip back to Amsterdam.

For our last night in Amsterdam we had arranged to meet up with a couple we had met previously in Sorrento on our previous trip. We attended a dinner show "Boom Chicago" and reminisced about the day we had spent together on Capri!

We walked to the train station the next morning, travelling to Schiphol Airport for our return flight to Canada and then on to Mexico. Our *balls* had been bouncing across Europe for five weeks. It was time to go *home.*

After returning from Europe, I got seriously hooked on blogging. I needed something to occupy my spare time of which there were lots! Summer doesn't really start until the end of June here when the Meridanos come to their summer homes at the beach. The snowbirds had picked up their *balls* and gone back home to the north just before we flew from Europe. I needed a project to keep me from wasting time on the computer all day long.

***

For those not familiar with blogging, it is more or less an online diary, journal, whatever you want it to be – complete with photographs if you choose. The concept is that you write, people read or subscribe, and then they see all of the entries you

171

post via the Internet or even Facebook if you choose. I was quickly addicted and proceeded to post-blog our European trip rather than sharing all 800 photos via some slideshow or online album. I became selective, obviously. The blog was simply entitled *Reg45's Blog.*

For the next six months I retravelled all of our destinations with explanations and links to places we visited. This blog is still accessible today for those who might be interested. The writer in me felt fulfilled!

I had also been encouraged by the success of my poetry book, *"Trust the Winds"*.

At every reading I was asked to explain the inspirational source of the poems – where was I? What was I thinking? Sensing a strong interest, I initiated a second blog www.trustthewinds.wordpress.com

I posted one poem from the book each week with a little background (as best I could remember). I also started a second volume of poetry. Shortly after I started I developed writer's block. An unfortunate comment from my spouse about a punctuation mark turned into the proverbial "kick in the balls". The writing stopped!

Since I was not writing ANYTHING I needed a new project. Copying an idea from my friend in the nearby city, I decided to start a men's club in Progreso. What started as a small group of friends has grown to over 100 guys who meet once a month for breakfast at a nearby hotel. There were no membership fees and NO speakers, nor did we sponsor any charitable works. Just camaraderie. Along with free membership comes regular news which I transmit online about events or happenings in the Yucatan. It became so successful that some of their wives asked to be added to the email list....I was writing something...

On the advice of another friend I started a third blog in 2011. I had received an email around Christmas asking to share a favorite cookie recipe. I know many have seen those. I chose not to participate, but the inspiration for a recipe blog formed in my mind. Many of our friends who have eaten with us seem to really enjoy our cooking, which is NOT typical Mexican. We are born and bred 'northerners' eh? The blog was called *Buen Provecho*, which is the Mexican way of saying enjoy your meal

To date I have had over 10,000 visitors and 350 plus recipes. Some day they may be available in book format.

At Easter in 2011, one of the ladies we met on the Danube River cruise came with a girlfriend to the Yucatan for a vacation. We were so honored to have them come to see the real Mexico as we call it. There were lots of laughs, lots of drinking wine and reminiscing about that trip! We have great memories of their visit!

Our long anticipated *Grape Escape* tour was slated for October 2011 and we began to make serious preparations once the ladies left. We would spend two weeks in California split between San Francisco and Napa Valley, and two weeks in British Columbia, split between Osoyoos and Victoria/Vancouver. The premise of the trip was, of course, to taste wines!!

We flew from Cancun to San Francisco in late fall, where we were met by our gay friends from the B and B where we had been married in Ontario in 2008. They had driven west, visiting friends along the way in Western Canada before heading south to San Francisco. The two of us had previously made a reservation at a B and B located in the Castro section, just off Market Street. Our friends stayed at an airport hotel using their rewards points.

For the first few days both couples explored the city on our own, travelling on the famous trolleys. As expected, the city was amazing. Everywhere we went we saw gay men – singles and couples, openly holding hands, embracing and kissing in the open. Obviously there are several million straight people who live in San Francisco, who for the most part were accepting of seeing two men together under such circumstances.

We had made no plans to meet any of the gay guys here. Perhaps we were intimidated just a little. Since this was probably a once in a lifetime trip, we insured that we see all of the tourist sites – *Golden Gate Bridge*, *COIT Tower*, *Ghirardelli Square*, *The Wharf*, *MOMA*, *Chinatown* and, of course the *Harvey Milk* statue at SF City Hall. Unfortunately, we were only able to walk half way across *Golden Gate Bridge* due to renovations.

Breakfast was included in our room. We were rather surprised to meet gay and straight couples there. It had a great atmosphere. When the owners were not onsite, the manager, a transsexual, was there to make sure everyone enjoyed their stays. Lunches and dinners were on the run during the day. There were lots of options in San Francisco, many of them in the gay district.

One evening our friends came in and joined us for dinner, after which we walked around the Castro like wide eyed children. It was surprisingly quiet – after all it was only 8 p.m. It was much like Church Street in Toronto – restaurants, trendy clothing stores, bars, the requisite sex shops and video stores. Actually it was not all that exciting…this was supposed to be the gay Mecca of the US. Next time we should go later at night I guessed. We could only wonder how many men's' *balls* had been dropped here over the years?

Towards the weekend, our friends picked us up at the B and B and we set out for Napa Valley where we had booked a unique B and B (timeshare) – our home base for this part of the trip.

By day we explored several wineries, sampling some great and not so great wines. Lunch was wherever we happened to be. Dinner was back at the timeshare, sharing whatever wines we had purchased that particular day. Since it was Canadian Thanksgiving, we decided to shop for a proper Thanksgiving dinner. Three of us were cooks which made it challenging in the small space. We ate outside on our patio – traditional turkey with stuffing, cranberries, mashed potatoes, squash, Brussels sprouts and pumpkin pie. All with just a small convection oven and four burners. We started with a great escargot appetizer while dinner was cooking AND a great bottle of Napa wine!

The other guys weren't feeling well the last couple of days while we were there, so they offered their vehicle for us to continue our wine touring over to Sonoma. At the end of the week we drove back to San Francisco, checking into the same B and B where we had been earlier on the trip. Over the last two days we explored as yet unseen sites – *Golden Gate Park* and *Haight-Ashbury*. The manager surprised me with a slice of birthday cake on the last night!

When it was time to leave San Francisco we headed to the airport for our flight to Vancouver, British Columbia. As in San Francisco, we planned to explore the city, this time renting a car for our drive to the Okanagan Valley – British Columbia Wine Country!

Our gracious hostess in Vancouver was our friend whom we had actually first met in Mexico through a mutual friend. Our actual destination was a timeshare we had visited a few years earlier – Osoyoos. We had been fortunate to book it ten months earlier. Spirit Ridge is a condo development nestled between the lake and the mountains complete with winery! This was to be our starting point for successive day trips to some of the one hundred or so wineries nearby. The winery at Spirit Ridge had begun as a venture by the Nk Mip First Nations Tribe. Subsequently it developed into a prestigious resort. Each day we would visit three or four wineries, sampling their wines and buying several bottles during our stay.

When we finally returned to Vancouver we headed across the Straits of Georgia to Vancouver Island where we were to meet an acquaintance in Nanaimo whom we had first met in Mexico two years previous, before spending a few days in the capital, Victoria.

Interestingly, we had communicated with a few guys on Gaydar once again, but we never actually connected with any while there!

At the end of the two weeks in BC we flew back to Mexico via Houston. Our thirty-two day adventure had come to an end. I would subsequently publish details of our trip on a new blog *Grape Escape*.

2012 was fast approaching, which meant many of the snowbirds would return to the Yucatan for the winter season. As was the norm, many new snowbirds would find their *balls* landing in Mexico for the first time.

This would be a year of extensive travel for us in Mexico and Canada. Our friend who had organized all of our previous group trips in Mexico decided to take a hiatus. Would we consider taking over on a trip to Chiapas? Since we had been before we were familiar with the itinerary – the archaeological site of *Palenque, Agua Azul, San Cristobal de las Casas, Canon*

Sumidero and *Villa Hermosa*. Our trusty friend Sergio would look after travel and lodging. All we had to do was advertise and collect the monies. Once the itinerary was finalized, I set out to pre-blog the trip – I was truly getting into this blogging! It was a great way to prepare our friends for the trip. The result was *Ay Chiapenecas*. We would be travelling by van so we limited ourselves to twenty-five fellow travelers.

The first day was a long ride to Palenque - eight hours! By the time we arrived it was late afternoon. Check in – unpack a bit – grab a quick dip in the pool and a drink, early dinner and then bed.

We had been to Palenque twice before, so while our group toured with Sergio, I sat in the Quadrangle and sought inspiration for my writing. Our friend worked on some sketches of the site, while mesmerized children watched her. Nearby others were selling trinkets…so common to the archaeological sites of Mexico.

That evening we walked into the town square for dinner. The next morning we were off to nearby Agua Azul waterfall before reaching our next destination of the day, the sites of *Bonampak* and *Yaxchilan*. The latter is only accessible by boat on the Usumacinta River separating Mexico from Guatemala. While we hear noises from the famous howler monkeys in Palenque, we actually got to see them in Yaxchilan! The final highlights of the day were the ancient Maya frescoes on the walls of Bonampak.

We returned to Palenque for another night at the hotel. Morning saw us boarding our van for the precarious trip to San Cristobal...

Actually, that road trip can best be described as precarious and treacherous. Chiapas being in the jungle, experiences lots of rain which subsequently wash out roads! We saw recent evidence of this, which caused us to change our plans as it was getting dark, and head directly to San Cristobal. All heaved sighs of relief as we reached our hotel. Thankfully, we were not returning by the same route. However, unknown to us there would be more adventures in the coming days...

SCLC is at an elevation of 2200 meters or 7200 feet. At best breathing can be difficult for the healthiest. With us were another couple who we knew might have difficulty with the altitude. Sure enough, on the second morning we had to call a doctor who diagnosed the husband with emphysema. I stayed behind for the day while the others day tripped to the nearby towns of San Juan Chamula and Zinacantán– very indigenous towns of great cultural traditions. These two I had seen previously.

At the end of the day, my spouse had to be treated by another doctor as a result of recent surgery on his wrist, when the stitches started to open up under the pressure.

That same evening, another member of the group contracted food poisoning after dining at a nearby restaurant. She and her husband chose to wait until the next day before returning by public transit to Merida, while the rest of us continued on.

We traveled on the next day with meds for our ailing friend and contact numbers for a doctor in Villahermosa should he require further medical attention.

En route we stopped for a boat tour of Canon Sumidero – one of Mexico's wonders. My ailing friend and I stayed behind while the rest sailed off in the motorboat. I had seen it before and was not terribly disappointed at staying at the dock.

We eventually reached Villa Hermosa where we had booked into a hotel, had dinner and went to bed – exhausted travelers!

On the final day of the trip we rose early, had breakfast and headed to *Parque La Venta* to see the famous Olmec sculptures and ruins. The Olmec had inhabited this area centuries before, whilst the Maya were in the Yucatan Peninsula.

By the time we got to La Venta, our ailing friend's wife was getting too tired to walk, so we got her a wheelchair and took turns pushing her along the gravel pathways. This trip had taken a toll on many of us, indeed! Our *balls* were hanging low...

Undoubtedly there was a sigh of relief once again as we boarded the bus for the long return trip to Merida and home...

***

Summer saw us spending five weeks in Canada, the longest we had been in Canada since coming to Mexico. We had many commitments – the first being to see our children and grandchildren! We had been away too long…

We flew direct from Cancun to Toronto where we were met by a friend who had recently come out after reading my first book. Early the next morning we got our rental car and started the first leg of our trip. Over the course of the next five weeks we would be in Cobourg (north of Toronto), Howe Island (one of the famous Thousand Islands), Kingston, Niagara-on-the-Lake, Cambridge, Waterloo, London and Windsor. It felt like such a whirlwind trip. Our last night we spent in Oakville with the ex-wife of the friend who had initially picked us up at the airport.

We seemed to always be eating out, unless we cooked for our friends. Normally, we always got together with my ex-wife and her partner. I had asked my spouse if we could have dinner with his ex-wife and her new husband, to which he agreed! I had met her briefly on two occasions but had not spent any time with her. I dashed off an email and they agreed to meet us for dinner at a nearby restaurant. Not surprisingly, we had a great time chatting. The ice was finally broken!! A few days later we flew back to Mexico…

Mexico has a long tradition on All Saints Day at the beginning of November. – *Dia de Los Muertos* – Day of the Dead. Cemeteries are decorated with thousands of yellow chrysanthemums, photos of the dead are displayed, candles are lit, favorite foods of the deceased are put out on an altar (including cerveza), while a nighttime vigil is conducted by the families. While celebrated throughout the country, it is best observed in Patzcuaro and Isla Janitzio in the state of Michoacán. With the intent of observing this first hand, we organized another trip of twenty-five friends to Mexico City, Teotihuacan and Morelia at the end of October. Of course, Sergio was our official guide.

Our group flew to Mexico City where we had booked the usual hotel near Teatro Bellas Artes. Since none of this group had been to Mexico City we visited the usual tourist attractions – Plaza Grande, Templo Mayor, National Anthropology Museum, Bellas Artes, Coyoacan, San Angel Market and Xochimilco again. It was better than the first time as we spent more time at each location. Indeed, we revisited Teotihuacan...

The *piece de raison* was, of course, the trip to Michoacán where we were booked into a quaint hotel in Patzcuaro for three nights. It was amazing just strolling the craft markets, as well as our visits to the nearby towns of Santa Clara de Cobre and Quiroga. The former is to brass what Taxco is to silver. The latter town is famous for *carnitas*, shredded pork cooked for hours and then shredded for sandwiches, Mexican style of course, in tortillas!

The real intent of our visit was to pay our respects at the cemeteries, primarily in Janitzio. We stopped en route to Tzintzuntzan at their cemetery. We purchased the traditional chrysanthemums which we draped on gravestones which were otherwise unattended by any family. It turned out to be more moving than the following nights visit to Janitzio!

The following day we walked around Patzcuaro before embarking on a boat for the trip to Janitzio around nine at night, crossing the waters with about forty other people. Most passengers were family members whose deceased family member was interred on the island.

As we approached the docks we could clearly see the candlelit cemetery at the shoreline with families paying homage. The stones of the cemetery are so crowded together that we were afraid to move for fear of stepping on them. We watched a dance display in an outdoor amphitheater which culminated in a lighted parade of fishing boats showing off their most unusual butterfly fishing nets. By midnight we were all ready to return to Patzcuaro and the comforts of our hotel.

The following morning we boarded our van for the trip back to Mexico City for two more nights. We had purchased tickets to the world famous *Ballet Folklorico* presentation at Bellas Artes to culminate the trip.

All of the Canadians caught an early morning flight to Toronto. The rest left later in the day for Merida.

***

In early 2012 I was approached by a Yucatecan doctor friend to see if I would be interested in meeting a married Cuban-American guy, now living in Cancun. Alonso had been coming to Merida for several months to take courses in psychotherapy at a local university on weekends. He and his wife and two teenaged children had been living in Cancun for a few years, where he was part of n outreach program operated by an agency in the US. His wife was also employed there.

Unbeknownst to her, he had begun to explore the possibility that he was actually gay. In his earlier years in the US he had encounters with other men, but eventually married, raising a family and pursuing his career.

When we first met he was in his mid forties. Our mutual doctor friend thought that I would make a good mentor for him as we shared similar stories – college, career, marriage, children – the social expectations for a young man.

After exchanging several emails we met at a restaurant near his college one weekend. While we were both very nervous, I played the role of a good listener while he told me his story. We both shed a few tears at that first meeting. He had told me he had known he might be gay in his early years, but being Catholic, he had repressed the idea. When they first moved to Mexico his life began to change. He and his wife were not getting along – one of the reasons he needed some time alone. While in Cancun he had met one or two guys but lived in fear that people at work might find out.

He was unknown in Merida. After his classes finished on the weekend, he began to explore the Merida gay scene (which is outwardly very limited). On the Merida chat sites he would eventually hook up with some guys. Every Sunday morning he would catch a bus back to Cancun to his family. This would be his routine for many months before we actually met. We continued to meet regularly after the restaurant, sometimes just touching base by phone or *WhatsApp.*

On occasion we would meet for a brief lunch while he was in Merida. By then my spouse had finally met Alonso. Our relationship was purely as friends – he came to call me Papa, since I was in my mid sixties and old enough to be his father.

Within the year he left his wife temporarily and came to live in Merida fulltime while he finished his studies, sharing a house with a female classmate.

There were several occasions where I visited him at his house where we continued to discuss our respective lives. He became my confidant and I his. We developed some real bonds. When he began to call me "Papa" I began to refer to him as "hijo" my son.

Ultimately he would come out to his family back in the States and then his children. He surmised that his wife also knew shortly after that. He left his job in Cancun, his home, his career, his livelihood and found a place to live in Merida.

He started to build a practice running out of his home, where he and his teenaged son were now living together. His daughter had gone back to the US. He continued to explore the gay community with no long term relationships in sight. He was barely surviving financially which made going out on a real date difficult. Of course, he was also suffering emotionally, a subject we continued to discuss regularly. His attraction to younger men almost half his age caused me much concern as I had gone down that road in the early stages of coming out.

Christmas 2012 was approaching and we would celebrate away from our families in Canada at Canadian friends nearby home with eighteen other foreigners – *expats* as they are called, who reside most of the year in Yucatan. New Years Eve was spent at another home with the same group with whom we had celebrated Christmas.

Our community had grown from the two of us in 2004 to approximately sixty people in the surrounding six blocks. Most were year round residents at this time, although we all maintained our Canadian citizenship. We represented Calgary, Winnipeg, Windsor, Montreal, and Kamloops. Wisconsin and Great Britain. Another couple from near Ottawa had recently purchased a home but was only wintering in Yucatan then.

We were not necessarily close knit, but we always let it be known amongst ourselves that this was indeed our new family – cousins in a sense – there for each other, but not living in each others space; after all, all of our *balls* had been dropped in this small seaside Mexican town, and for the most part we knew we would ultimately die here. None of us ever harbored thoughts of returning north, with the exception of brief vacations.

We were destined to play all of our *balls* here, of that there was no doubt!

***

2013 saw us travelling again to Mexico City as well as spending a week in Puerto Vallarta with friends from Minnesota who we had met a few years earlier in Merida.

One of our closest friends brought his elderly mother here from Canada to live, but she passed away within the month unfortunately. This was our first experience dealing with the death of someone in the Yucatan. When I got the call in early morning I quickly went to their home. Mother has passed in her sleep after a short period of hospitalization. She had been discharged only a day before after being treated for an intestinal ailment.

The hospital sent a doctor to make the official pronouncement. We called the local funeral home who arrived promptly to take her body away... John was in Progreso at the time. Since he spoke Spanish he went with our friend to make all of the necessary arrangements for cremation. He also went to the crematorium to witness the occurrence. Less than eight hours after she had passed, the cremation was complete. Early the next day the ashes were received. Death is handled very expeditiously in Yucatan unless it results from an accident or crime.

We lost our dear friend, the owner of the B and B where we had been married back in Ontario in 2008. He was only fifty-nine years old.

Additionally, we added to our group of friends with a couple from Florida – she an Army nurse and he a helicopter pilot during the Vietnam War.

Another addition was a gay couple from Texas, more recently Hawaii, as well as a lesbian couple. Another Canadian couple was in the process of building their dream home here as well once he had retired from work in Calgary.

Our social circle now included friends, some only part time, from Ohio, Massachusetts, Oregon, Michigan, the Carolinas, England, California, Wisconsin, Colorado, Germany, Ontario, Quebec, Nova Scotia, etc.

In 2014 we organized a long dreamed of trip to Cuba, spending ten days in Havana, Pinar del Rio, Cienfuegos and Trinidad de Cuba. Our group of 25 intrepid travelers included some of my spouse's relatives who flew in from Canada to join us. Sergio was once again our man!

It was a great adventure! We discovered Havana or Habana as the locals pronounce it, visiting a previous home of Ernest Hemingway, *La Finca*. In Pinar del Rio we saw the tobacco fields and *mogotes* – limestone mountains. From there we travelled east to Cienfuegos and Trinidad del Cuba.

Our last days in Havana were spent going to see the Buena Vista Social Club, touring in classic cars from the 60's and seeing a floorshow at Hotel Nacional. During the time we were walking around the city center, we were under the watchful eyes of younger Cuban men – *pingueros*, - young men more than willing to engage male foreigners in sexual activity for a price! Many were not gay, simply earning a living, returning to their wives or girlfriends after a few hours of well paid work each day – if they were lucky.

John went north to see his son in Calgary that spring, while I remained in Yucatan only to join him a week later in Toronto. We both got time to spend with our children and grandchildren. A special occasion was an afternoon lunch with my cousins whom I had not seen inn over 50 years!! Time does truly fly. The wonders of *Facebook*.

In late summer, our friend offered to rent us a new house he was having built just around the corner from our current place. We were offered input on the design and he allowed us to design our dream kitchen since we both love to cook. In all fairness we designed and paid for the kitchen as a gesture of goodwill...

I cannot help but wonder what two Canadian farm boys ever did to deserve this new opportunity. And so that June we moved into the new house, likely the last place our *balls* would ever drop. Appropriately we named it in Mayan

"Üh T'zok Nahji" which means the last dwelling place!

It was wonderful. For the first time since moving to Mexico 10 years earlier, we had complete privacy. We loved our dream kitchen, our heated swimming pool, and our outdoor living space. We could finally entertain our many friends, celebrating Christmases and New Years in our own home. We were living a dream!

The day after we moved in we were off to Ontario again for five weeks. At the end of the trip my youngest daughter and her youngest daughter joined us for the flight back to Mexico for a ten day visit – their first. Of course, we introduced them to our *cousins...*

The following summer my oldest granddaughter and her father's sister visited us in Mexico. For two weeks. I took a bus to Cancun to meet them both and we bussed back to Progreso. We had a great time with them visiting the ruins, sleeping at our friends B and B in the jungle, and riding in a caliche in Merida one evening. Most of the time was spent in our swimming pool and eating out. When time came for them to depart, we took them back to Cancun by car, staying overnight and touring the area.

During that same summer we had met two guys online, Rogelio from Veracruz and Bernard from Tabasco who were moving to Merida and looking for new friends to play cards. I responded on Facebook and we met a week or so later. They were both in their early 30's, gay and partnered.

Neither had jobs, but the younger had previously been working in the Middle East. His job paid him well and he had saved enough money for a new house here. Initially we had met for coffee and then we invited them to the beach one afternoon to swim and have dinner. Only the younger guy spoke English se we had some challenged communicating with his partner. We all got along very well and their visits became more frequent. Money was tight for them and entertainment wasn't in their budget; they brought dessert, we cooked dinner and supplied the wine. On hotter days we enjoyed the pool together. When it got colder, we turned on the pool heater. After a few visits we suggested they spend the night rather than drink and drive. They gratefully accepted. Our social circle expanded. Of course, we enjoyed the company of two younger guys! Our *balls* were met to meet...

That same year, we were asked to help out with a Silent Auction for the local ladies group. Our job was to gather items for the auction from nearby merchants. The ladies knew full well that we had many connections after living here twelve years! The event would be part of their annual fashion show to raise money for school children.

At the same time we were arranging a group tour to Oaxaca for fifteen friends who would be in the area for the winter. Between these two activities we were kept very busy.

The snowbird season had begun. It always brought mixed feelings. We had many local expat friends who live here full time. The onslaught each season sees the return of some special seasonal friends and hordes of new ones. Those coming for the first time present challenges – they don't do their homework before choosing Progreso – too many dogs – too much garbage – the Gulf isn't as beautiful as the Caribbean – I don't understand the language – where are all of the foods we had back in the North??? After twelve years living here we had heard it all before...*ad nauseum*.

The social life here multiplies every winter. The local expat hotels revved up their activities. On some nights, reservations were required. Part of the seasonal problem is that the snowbirds generally do not have or rent cars. They don't travel into the city at night using the frequent busses. Most events in the city started at 8 pm. Snowbirds eat, drink and shop locally. They can often be found hanging out with the cruise ship passengers at any of several watering holes. They tend not to cook at home. Their *balls* may have been dropped here, temporarily, but many aren't willing to play them well...

In lieu of Christmas and New Years dinners at our house we decided to throw a pre-Christmas party. We modelled it after a *charcuterie* event that my spouse's daughter in law had at her home when we had lasted visited in Canada. Day by day the guest list grew until we hit sixty-five! Fortunately the weather was great and we managed to feed all of our guests quite well. Gay guys do like to throw parties!

Christmas dinner was a quieter affair at our landlords place nearby with just our close friends. New Year's saw us at another friends home nearby with a potluck dinner just before midnight. It had been quite a year.

The Fashion Show/Silent Auction was a huge success in spite of the rain and high winds which threatened our tents and auction items. In the end we quadrupled their previous intake of monies, thanks to the generosity of the sponsors we sought out. Of course we have been asked to do it again. Unfortunately, the culmination of the fundraiser saw four of our close friends leaving Progreso. Their *balls* were heading north in the case of one couple (for medical reasons) – the other couple headed to Puerta Vallarta on the west coast. Other new couples would replace them.

As for the Oaxaca trip, it was now just one week away...

Just before we left on the trip my oldest granddaughter gave birth to my great granddaughter. When she had first told me about being pregnant I was not happy. She was only nineteen years old and had only finished high school. When she had visited us the previous summer with an aunt, she had not said a word about this. It was only after she returned to Canada that she announced *on Facebook* by way of an ultrasound that she and her boyfriend were expecting! As much as I would like to have been there, it was not possible with our pending trip.

In late 2015 we had sent out feelers about the trip. We had planned on flying into Mexico City and travelling by van to Oaxaca and Puebla. We cut off the numbers at fifteen people. Sergio once again handled the logistics of travel and accommodation.

We spent seven days together. During the three days together in Oaxaca we visited the archaeological sites of *Monte Alban* and *Mitla*, sipped mescal, observed the making of wool carpets, and visited local craft centers where they made the whimsical *alebrijes* wooden figures. We purchased a fair amount of the Oaxacan black pottery as well.

In Puebla we visited the Cathedral, the Capilla de Rosario and the nearby pyramid at Cholula, actually the largest in the world!

Back in Mexico City we visited Frida Kahlo's Casa Azul, the San Angelo Artists Bazaar and Xochimilco (fourth time). These trips took their toll on our older friends AND ourselves. We decided that the next trip we would again be on our own...no more groups.

My milestone 70th birthday was October 15, 2015. For several moths, we had been watching the Dutch violinist/concert master, *Andre Rieu* on PBS. He was the conductor for the Johann Strauss Orchestra. Coincidentally he was coming to Mexico City at the same time and John managed to get us tickets on my birthday. As if that wasn't enough reason to go, he also planned a sunrise, hot air balloon over the Aztec ruins at Teotihuacan. This would be our very first trip on our own after all of the previous group tours! Friends had told us about a wonderful B and B in Condesa, an art deco neighbourhood, which we booked for the stay. The B and B was owned by an American-Mexican gay couple and it more than lived up to its reputation as the number one B and B in Mexico City! Our hosts were charming and certainly made all of their guests feel at home. Every night they had a two hour Happy Hour. Breakfasts were incredible. The mixed staff of gay and straight men and women were very accommodating to ay request, going so far as to arrange the hot air balloon trip and securing the concert tickets before our arrival. In the evening of my birthday they had a four hour Happy Hour and brought in a small group of musicians to play for my birthday! A few of the ladies who prepared breakfast every morning came back to prepare some light snacks for the event. Men danced with men and women danced with men. The young Mexican owner and a couple of the male employees even dragged me onto the dance floor! We were told afterwards that this was the first time that previous guests had ever seen them have a party. We had somehow connected...

After this wonderful experience we vowed that we would go back again as often as possible.

***

In the summer of 2016 we headed north for a five week trip to Ontario and Quebec. Aside from our respective families, we had numerous snowbird friends who spent the spring and summers there. We were also to attend the wedding of the son of my spouse's half sister. He and his fiancée had been with us on the trip to Cuba. We arrived one week before the wedding to visit our families and

195

then set out towards Quebec. Along the way we stopped in Kingston where we visited friends from my spouse's university days. From there we were off to Montreal to visit with a woman from Progreso and her Canadian husband. During our stay we went south to meet up with friends from Vermont for a lovely dinner in Ste. Jean Richelieu, Quebec.

Leaving there, we headed into the Gatineau region to visit with our neighbours from Progreso who owned a house on the lake near Wakefield. The next day we headed west to Ottawa, where we were to spend a few days playing tourist. A woman friend we knew from Progreso had married a guy from Texas and she met us in Ottawa where she was attending her nieces wedding. Coincidence? Upon second thought I remembered that a long ago friend from Windsor had moved to Ottawa with her second husband. One phone call later and we decided to meet for diner that night at a lovely old pizza place that was very well known locally.

The rest of the time we explored Ottawa, the Parliament Buildings, the Canadian History Museum, etc. The highlight was the Sound and Light Show at Parliament Hill one night.

In nearby Burnstown on our way back to Peterborough we met up with another snowbird couple we knew from Progreso. They were both artists and owned a lovely and quaint property where they graciously allowed us to stay.

We eventually made it back to Toronto where we spent the night at an airport hotel before flying to spend a week with another couple outside of Sault Ste. Marie. They actually owned a small farm about twenty minutes from the city. Both were avid sailors and, of course, we had to go sailing at least once. With us onboard they competed in a sailboat race on the St. Mary's River, dodging mammoth lake freighters.

One week on the farm was idyllic, since we were both farm boys originally...

Too soon we flew back to Toronto and then the next morning caught an early flight back to Mexico.

Our next planned trip in the fall took us back to Mexico City with two Canadian friends whom we had known for quite a few years in Progreso. We were sitting at a restaurant in early July when they asked if we had any plans to return to Cuba. Unfortunately, we didn't have any plans at that time, but we offered that we were going back to The Red Tree House in Mexico City for my 71st birthday. They looked at each other and both jumped in, "Could we go with you?"

So, come October, the four of us were off to Mexico City for another adventure! We flew from Merida on an early morning flight, arriving in Mexico City around noon. Since we were travelling light, my spouse felt we could take the Metro this time. Why do I always go along with that idea? I hate travelling from the airport on the subway! It isn't faster than a taxi with all of the route changes. Yeah, its free for us seniors! Most of the time the escalators do not work, which leaves those long, dirty staircases...grr.

We persevered and soon reached the B and B. It was the same as always, very welcoming! Our rooms were not ready so we decided to go across the street for lunch. One thing we LOVE about Mexico City is the variety of foods from all over Mexico. We had no specific plans during our stay so we decided to book one of the many food tours for later in the week. This day we would simply walk the streets of Condesa, exploring its lovely neighborhood. We arrived back in time for a brief rest, followed by the traditional Happy Hour with the other guests. When it was over we walked to one of the may nearby restaurants with another couple whom we met at Happy Hour. Lights out!

The next morning we arrived at breakfast with the other guests. As last time, there was the regular buffet of fruits, cereal, breads, juices and yogurt. The coffee is great! Each day the kitchen staff prepare one special Mexican dish served hot in addition to the buffet. One day it might be chilaquiles. Another day empanadas. If you stay a full week you will ever have the same hot dish. Breakfast goes on quite awhile, as other guests arrive and the conversation flows. Then the day gets started. This day we were headed to San Angelo for the artists market. *Uber* does it!

This event is held every Saturday in the square with hundreds of artists and other vendors of pottery, blankets, etc. We went our separate ways, exploring all that was on display. This was not our first time here, so we managed to see a lot of things but bought nothing...lol. Before we knew it, it was time for lunch on the square at a wonderful restaurant! Satiated, it was once again Uber time! Back to the B and B...R and R, Happy Hour and another restaurant...

The following day was our scheduled Food Tour. The four of us got on the Metro to head downtown where we met our guide – a young woman in her twenties who had spent time in many parts of Mexico. Our first stop was a Oaxacan restaurant where we sampled a margarita and an empanada filled with *huitlacoche*. The latter is like a Scottish pasty filled with black corn fungus. Ok...it tastes like mushrooms, but is black. On the farm in Canada we always cut the fungus off and threw it away. Who knew it was edible?

Our next stop was the very well-know San Juan Mercado. It is one of the premier mercados in Mexico City for top chefs who work at the best restaurants. We sampled some great Mexica cheeses, drank some Mexica wine, explored the wild meats food stall where we sampled ants and termites, had a nice little lunch of wild boar, ending up at a fantastic fruit and vegetable stall where we sampled all kinds of very fresh items we ever see in Yucatan. The highlight was the freshly made chocolate ice cream (helado) with a very fresh smelling rose bud. It was ALL edible!

Our tour continued on foot to a street vendor, one of the first families to operate in Mexico City. The caldo de camarones (shrimp soup) was steaming hot and very delicious. Despite a little drizzle we continued our walk. All along the way our guide told us a little more about the history of places, until we ended up in the Zocalo (main square). By now we had been touring about three hours. Can you say *cantina*?

The next two stops were at a very traditional cantina where they did not use to allow women. The other cantina was destroyed during the famous earth quake and had been rebuilt by the government to encourage rebuilding in Centro. It actually had a small theatre where performers would come by in the evenings.

Our last stop of the day was the oldest candy store in Mexico City where we sampled and bought some delicious candy. After over four hours, it was UBER time again! NO more walking...

Back at the B and B we collapsed and awaited Happy Hour! No one even wanted to think of dinner!!! Early to bed...

Several years ago, my oldest daughter forwarded a YouTube video to me – *Life on a Train* (which appears to have been removed from YouTube). The gist of the presentation was that throughout our lives we are passengers on a train. People get on and get off along the journey for various reasons.

We have been blessed on our journey by many passengers – some have been with us a brief time, some have left this Earth, others have stayed longer, some we have not yet met! Will any be with us when the journey ends?

Only the Universe knows when or where our *balls* will finally drop.

What are the reasons why some left the Yucatan while others remained?

1. Many could not accept the cultural and language differences.
2. Many jumped in to purchase properties without a full appreciation for the economics of remodeling a house and property.
3. Many could not accept being so far removed from families and friends – children and grandchildren.
4. Many were disillusioned when they could not have in Mexico what they had in the US and Canada.
5. Many wanted Mexico and the Mexicans to be more like the US and the Americans.
6. Some were concerned about the rising evidence of drugs and gangs in the Yucatan.

7. Some left when the economies of the US and Canada collapsed and they could no longer afford two residences – one in the north and one in Mexico.
8. Some left when their health began to fail.

Those whose *balls* remained here, did so because –

1. They accepted life in the Yucatan for what it was – a safe, tranquil place removed from the hectic pace of life in the north.
2. They willingly attempted to learn the language and customs of the Yucatan, as well as the culture.
3. They had no great desire to be part of American society. Many were retirees with adequate pensions as well.
4. They had similar spiritual values which allowed them to live in the present and accept what life offered on a daily basis.
5. They were no longer willing to be associated with the right-wing government under George W. Bush and/or the following government of Barack Obama and the reality of newly-elected President Donald Trump!
6. They were very liberal and open-minded in general.
7. They had sufficient incomes which allowed them to live more comfortably and more affordably than they could in the north.
8. They developed circles of friends – like minded people – which allowed them to feel less isolated.

9. They immersed themselves in Mexico, choosing not to live in gated communities, separate from the real Mexicans.

John and I were committed to spending the rest of our days here. I had jokingly told his younger son that if anything happened to his father while we were here, that I would have him cremated and sent back to Canada in a *piñata* so he could beat the hell out of his Dad, no doubt releasing all those pent up emotions he has carried around all these years! I exaggerate….his son harboured no animosity!

At this moment in time I could never imagine our *balls* ever leaving this country, for any reason.

Then again, who of us living here would ever have imagined our *balls* being dropped here so late in life?

And where are they now?

THE CANADIANS

Dani and Chad

Dani and Chad ultimately divorced. Both sons are with their father in Canada. Chad found work in Canada – dreams of the Far East have faded. Dani has no intention of returning to Canada and recently started a property management business catering to gringos. Most recently she had been seeing a middle aged American socially. At this writing she has relocated to the US and remarried. Her youngest son has made her a grandmother!

Jack

Jack and his new partner continued to live in the US after their marriage in Canada in 2006. Jack became an ordained minister. Recently he accepted a job in Ontario as a counselor and they did move to Ontario where his partner now has Canadian citizenship. We hoped that someday they would visit us in Progreso. In September 2008, Jack was the minister at our wedding! Jack started a new church in Ontario. His partner also went into the Ministry, but a different denomination. In the last two or three years we have very little communication with them...

Anna

Anna's restaurant is doing very well. She has gotten established on the tourist route to Uxmal. She built another two palapas on her property for visitors. Two Christmases in a row we organized a group of 35 "snowbirds" for a traditional Christmas dinner. She has expanded the restaurant to include a personal residence and a swimming pool. She remains unattached but has developed several female friends near her restaurant. Her business continues to thrive to where she now has eight rental units. The B and B is listed for sale, but she is in no hurry to sell now that she has a local Yucatecan manager. She built herself a studio on the property in 2015. In early 2016 she bought a beachfront condo unit along the coastline where she goes for peace and quiet, while still operating the B and B.

THE AMERICANS

Tom and Frank

Frank's ninety-nine year old mother passed away as this book was initially wrapping up. Life changed for them. They sold the infamous beachfront condo and renovated a beach house closer to Progreso. Tom was into property management and spent a lot of time away from the house. Frank and Tom were frequent visitors to gay chat rooms in the city. Their city home was sold. We did spend Thanksgiving 2008 with them and a group of friends and also celebrated Tom's 60th birthday with them in the city.

At the celebration were many of their friends whom we knew. Surprisingly, the young architect, Arturo was there...THE Arturo with whom John had had a relationship before I met him.

In 2009 Tom and Frank went their separate ways. Tom moved into their beach house while Frank purchased another home in the city, soon finding another partner half his age! Tom started hanging out with the wrong crowd. After bringing one home one night, he was found unconscious, near death by a close friend who lived nearby. His car had been stolen and his house was locked *from the outside*. Once fully recovered, he sold the beach house. Moving back to a small house in the city. He started seeing more questionable, young men.

Tragically, Tom was found murdered in his home in 2012. The crime has yet to be solved. Frank has found a new, younger love at this writing and has built a new home outside the city.

Ross and Marianne

After their divorce, Marianne took Ross' son back to Texas; Ross continued to live in Progreso building houses for gringos. He moved to Playa del Carmen to manage a hotel property. He still only dated younger women less than 25 years of age. We had thought that *Peter Pan may* never grow up.

Sadly, Ross was killed in Playa del Carmen in a motorcycle accident in 2012, shortly after he had remarried.

George and Alyce

George and Alice continued to live in North Carolina, where George was supposedly teaching at a university. They continued to own Casa Henequen, which was rented by a film crew in the summer of 2007. The film is about a Mexican girl who goes to the US for Spring Break and comes back to Mexico pregnant. Just maybe their own daughter was the inspiration for the writer of that film? They finally sold their hotel in 2015.

Ralph

Ralph separated from Don and is now retired. When Don moved to his condo in Puerta Vallarta, Ralph purchased the house outside Chicago. He still resides there with his beloved dog. He recently became a grandfather.

Terry

Terry and his partner found their retirement villa in Guatemala. His HIV status remains the same. He retired in March 2008. His partner's father died at Christmas. We exchange regular emails. In late spring of 2008 we were surprised by a week long visit from him. He stayed with us in NA while looking for additional investment property here. We felt an instant connection with him from the moment he stepped off the airplane in Cancun. In December 2008, I flew to Orlando to spend two days with him and his partner. I had the opportunity to meet his family before I flew north to Detroit. Terry's father passed away in 2016.

Chas and Emily

After a wedding in Bali they returned to Amsterdam, moving back to the US after the birth of their second child. We are in touch with regular emails at holiday time.

James

James is presumably still a tour guide in Rome and still searching for Mr. Right. He keeps in touch with his ex-wife and continues to see his young children regularly. We rarely exchange emails anymore, except for holidays. In 2010 we returned to Rome where we caught up with him once again. He had recently broken up with yet another partner. Instead of hiring him as a tour guide, we opted for a night of wine bar hopping, just the three of us. Once again we had a great time, purely platonic.

Bob

Bob quit his job in Italy to return to the US to manage another property in the southwest, but only after one last fling with Raoul we surmise!

Alonso

Alonso is still single, but his counselling sessions with his clients have made him financially more pleased. We still chat regularly at least every other day. His son still lives in Merida. Just recently his older daughter flew down from the US for a visit.

THE ITALIANS

Paolo

Lacking email, Paolo is believed to be running his wonderful restaurant outside Siena,

Italy. His restaurant appeals to a wide clientele of local Italians who appreciate exquisite food.

Davide

We suspect that Davide continues to run his restaurant behind the Milan train station, catering to mainly gay clientele.

Stefano

Although we had a few emails from Stefano after we returned from Italy, he was last known to still be making regular trips to visit his boyfriend in Venice.

Raoul

He was last seen hustling in the streets of Milan, saving money to send to his teenaged wife and their infant son in Romania, just before Bob left Italy and returned to the US.

THE BRITS

Willie

Willie, tragically, lost his father six months before this book was initially completed. We see him from time to time at a local Irish pub we visit in Merida. He belongs to a newly established Polo Club outside Merida. Willie has become an incredible photographer! In 2017, we celebrated his 50th birthday with him, his wife and friends at a popular extrañero restaurant in Merida. One of his paintings hangs in our home.

THE MEXICANS

Alberto

Since we first met Alberto he has been working as an architect in the nearby city. It was a struggle getting him through the program, but we stayed on his case. He introduced us to his mother several years ago when she came to visit him. Our contact has grown more distant as he grows older and is in a better place financially than when he was young and struggling. We get messages from time to time, usually on our birthdays or holidays. He is still single as far as we know…

Rogelio and Bernard

Although we used to get together at least once a month, we have grown apart. Two years ago, Bernard called me early one morning on Easter Sunday. He had found out that Rogelio had been meeting with other guys when he was supposed to be at work. He was shattered. They had bought a house together. I went to his home to try and console him as best I could, as it seemed like the relationship was broken. After a few weeks they got back together, but we never saw the two of them together in Progreso again for a year or so. Bernard would visit while Rogelio was working on Sundays. Eventually Bernard asked if he could bring Rogelio to the beach and we gave in. It was difficult to forgive Rogelio for what had occurred and how he had hurt Bernard. We decided that if Bernard was able to do so, then so should we. After that visit we rarely saw them again. Our relationship with them was irreparably damaged.

Andreas

Andreas was still finding his way. Now out to his family, he had a steady boyfriend who was a teacher in a nearby pueblo. He continued to live here with his aging grandmother until the fall of 2008 when he graduated and got a job teaching Spanish culture in the Far East. The relationship with his boyfriend floundered and he met a young Spanish student while teaching, who also happened to be gay. We ended up mentoring his former boyfriend at this point in time. He eventually moved on. In the interim Andreas and his new BF moved to Spain where they eventually entered into a Civil Union. Once married they began travelling in Europe, whenever they had time off working, together. They did briefly return to Mexico, before finally settling in England.

Made in the USA
Columbia, SC
14 July 2018